UPCYCLE WITH DECOUPAGE

About the Author/Artist

I live in the country and have been working with Decoupage for over 20 years. I've sold in boutiques in my home state of New Jersey and in the state of Pennsylvania. I have a shop on Etsy called Hydrangeapath and a Facebook page with the same name. My very supportive husband has always been beside me helping me to move forward when I feel those "discouraged artist blues" coming on. His knowledge of anything business has helped me tremendously with my anything creative nature.

We are forever taking in strays, whether they are dogs and cats or birds, turtles or baby bunnies. All are welcome here.

My love of creating comes from my Mother who we lost a few years ago. Anyone who has lost a parent, knows the very heavy time in life you go through after that happens. Yet, I could always hear her encouraging me to finish this book. She was my best friend and I continue to talk to her for support and help and she always manages to bring me comfort still.
I'm very close to my brothers and my father and a few close friends. We have a large family and I can say that I genuinely like and get along with all of them. I'm very lucky to have been born into such a loving family. I am also lucky enough to have a loving and supportive family of inlaws.

I've been a member of the Decoupage Guild (Decoupage Artists Worldwide) for several years and find them a very good resource when I myself get stuck or need some inspiration.

TABLE OF CONTENTS

Foreword

There is just so much you can do with decoupage. I have decoupaged so many items that I would have otherwise thrown out. I've decoupaged several items that perhaps you may have thrown out. I have made gifts, house ware products- all serving a purpose, suitcases, floral vases, votives for my candles, and then? I have made some products just for fun or beauty. I have found this to be a craft that is very easy on the change purse, since most of the supplies are very inexpensive, and a lot of the projects are items that you have on hand-but you just don't know what to do with. It can also be quite elegant since you get to select the themes of what you want to do. It's easy to learn, the most difficult part may be the cutting and that just requires that you are careful and take your time. The best pair of scissors for the job cost ten dollars at the craft store, and with the 40 percent off coupon so readily available on line or in your newspaper you can even get those for a good price. You can take your own pictures and make projects for gifts, or your home. That favorite picture of your child, dog, cat or other family member? You can make something lovely out of that, display it and be proud that you were the one who made it.

There are endless ideas for themes, gifts and party decorating. Organizing, storing, and most important to me, beautifying your home. I want to give you the easiest instructions, and attempt to simplify the process.

You can choose whichever project you want to work on first, there is no order and they don't get progressively harder or easier. Although as with most anything you do, the more you do them, the easier they become. It is not a difficult craft to begin with. Even children can do it. They (like me) love getting all gooey and messy. Which reminds me, I have several old T-shirts, and a few beat up pairs of pants that I will wear to do this work. It can get messy and gooey and any outfit that you would paint in would be perfect for decoupage.

It helps to re use old baby food jars if you have them on hand. If you buy a large container of decoupage glue - or make your own   (I'll tell you how) the glue can start to get lumps in it, dust, pieces of the sponge brush or lint and you may feel compelled then to throw it out. Instead, pour an amount into a baby food jar. It will be good for the project at hand. And with that small of an amount you will not get all the particles that can end up showing up on your project.

Sometimes, I can get wordy when I'm describing something. In my attempt to be thorough, I may be too verbose when you would prefer a bottom line instruction. This page is a quick reference guide to all of the projects. There may be other steps depending on the project, but the following steps and supplies are needed for all of the projects.

Supplies:

- Small curved decoupage scissors. (Available at any craft store)
- Shallow bowl of water (must be large enough to fit your image in - I use the Styrofoam containers that normally hold your grocery meats. I wash them with bleach and dish washing liquid first. Though any shallow bin for holding an inch of water would work fine.
- Decoupage glue   (available in matt, semi gloss or high gloss)
- You can also mix your own using regular old white glue with wallpaper paste. I've included the recipe for making your own glue below.
- Lint Free cloth
- Topcoat. There are waterproof topcoats as well as topcoats that protect from UV rays. Flat, semi gloss and gloss. Decide if the item you are working on will be outdoors in sunlight or humid conditions, or inside. Base your topcoat choice on that.
- Cardboard nail files, strongest grit. Usually used on acrylic nails.
- A hard brayer
- Automotive wet/dry sanding paper
- Any of the following to use as your decoupage project;
- Photo's that you have made copies of. (These must be laser copies and not copies from the ink jet printers most of us have at home.)
- Greeting cards, wrapping paper, napkins, tissue paper, wallpaper, phone book pages, foreign books, old books, water color images. You could actually paint a watercolor image; make a few copies of it and decoupage with it. Making it truly, your work of art.

I have tried using some tricks on the ink jet prints. I've tried top coating them, heating them in the oven for 20 minutes at 200 degrees, and even putting a light layer of hairspray over them. All of my work still ran. I was trying to save myself a trip to the copy store and possibly stumble along some new way to use ink jet prints without any running. None of them worked. Oh well. One day I'll get a laser printer for my house. (The cost of ink cartridges is very high but you get a lot more copies for your money.)

And here are the basic instructions for all of the projects.

- Tear or cut your papers.
- Lay them out first while dry on your surface to see how they will look.
- Apply decoupage glue to area of item you are going to lay the image on.
- Dip image in water. Shake the excess water off of the image then dab on a lint free cloth to dry it out.
- Place wet image over surface area where you just applied decoupage glue.
- Use a brush or brayer to smooth out air bubbles. On round or lumpy surfaces such as with Paper Mache you will want to use a sewing needle to pierce bubbles.
- Repeat above steps for each image you are applying. Let dry.
- Apply more coats of decoupage glue. (Between 5 and 20 depending)
- Dry then sand lightly between coats. Dust your piece off and top coat!

That is how you decoupage in a nutshell. There are other additions that we'll learn along the way. Using tissue papers, markers, glitters, 3-D paints, acrylic paints and perhaps a few specialty paints.

And here is a recipe for making your own decoupage glue.

You will mix equal amounts of *clear* wallpaper glue with any white craft glue. White craft glue would be any glue like Elmer's. A store will normally sell a generic brand right next to the Elmer's glue. Make sure you purchase wallpaper glue that dries clear. It will say "Dries Clear" on the label. If it doesn't say this, do not get it. I had a hardware store employee tell me that they all dried clear, which I found out the hard way, is not true.

You can make any amount of the glue that you like. I started with a glass spaghetti jar, added the white craft glue up to the half way mark, and then added the wallpaper paste. I did have to spoon the wallpaper paste out since it's a bit on the gelatinous side. Stir it all together once, and you don't need to mix it again. This gives you the flattest finish possible. I prefer to start with a flat finish. As the piece looks more finished I decide if I want to give it a glossier look. The topcoat can either remain a matte finish or you can go with a slightly shinier look with the satin. Gloss will give you the shiniest of all finishes.

Glass Votives

This is where it all started for me. The plain clear glass votives are inexpensive, easy to work on, and can be made to look quite elegant. You can dress them up or stop once you are done decoupaging them. I'll give you instructions and ideas for doing the accessorized option so you can choose to continue with the project or simply stop once you have applied your papers.

Most of us love candles and there are so many lovely colors of tissue papers available today. You can also use Mulberry or rice paper. In my area I have needed to go to an art supply store or a better stationery store to get the rice paper or mulberry paper. You can also use plain white tissue paper (the kind you purchase to go inside gift bag) and rubber stamp over it. Make sure you are using ink based stamped pads since the water based ones will run as soon as you decoupage them. You can use embossing powder if you like, or colored markers or pencils if you are good at that. I'm creative and artistic yet each time I've tried to color inside my rubber-stamping project it just doesn't look as nice as the picture on the front of the rubber stamp. Again, just make sure your pencils and markers are waterproof.

Before you get started, you'll want to choose a theme. It's springtime here in the northeast and I like the soft look of candles going up the stairs in our foyer. I wanted a nice springtime theme. So I purchased pink tissue paper and some faux miniature branches of Cherry Blossoms. I also experimented with the tiny silk roses you get in the wedding section of the craft store.

You may want to put some votives around your bathtub. You may just want a simple candle in your bathroom. Do you have a beach themed bathroom? Would you like some shells, twine and sand for your votives? Or do you have a country look in your home? You may want some miniature pieces of fruit to decorate the votive, with some raffia tied around it. You can also rubber stamp something onto tissue paper. Do you like shabby chic? There are so many varieties of tiny flowers available; you only need to stick to the color theme of shabby chic. (Very light pinks, creams and soft green/any pastels will do but the strongest color theme in shabby style seems to be the first 3 colors I mentioned) Look through any web site with shabby chic in the title and you'll notice the strong patterns of roses, with pinks, creams and whites.

Do you want these votives to go in front of each dinner plate for a holiday party you are throwing? You can do a theme and offer the votives as a gifts to each guest, or you can keep them for next year since the holiday will come around again. Do you have a porch? You can line these around the floor of your porch for that summer party that goes into the evening hours. *Make sure to use an outdoor topcoat in this case.

Once we get started you will start to come up with some new ideas of your own. And if you don't know yet what you want to do, we can still start to decoupage. As you are working on the project an idea will come to you. Perhaps my idea will inspire you and you may want to just follow my instructions and complete this project.

Since you will be doing more than one of these votives you will always be drying one while working on the next one. I always place my work near a heat vent in the fall/winter season for quicker drying, and in direct sunlight inside during the spring and summer months.

Here's what we will need:

- Glass votives (available at any craft store) approx. 2 inches tall
- Tissue paper (any color(s) you want /Available in craft stores (note that you can not use actual tissues since they will fall apart.)
- Decoupage glue
- Topcoat or sealer (make sure to use an outdoor sealer if these are going outside)

- Sheet of matching felt with sticky back for base of votive
- Trinkets: This would include shells, glitter, buttons, flowers, etc.
- Sponge brushes (more than one) the one-inch size works fine.
- Long sheet of wax paper
- Nail file (coarse cardboard type from drug or beauty store)
- Velvet Ribbon or Raffia

1. Before we start, take a sheet of your tissue paper and tear the hard straight edge off all sides. There should be no hard edges left anywhere on your paper. Discard the torn edges.

2. Now, tear the sheet of tissue paper into several small pieces of any shaped portions but try to keep them all less than two inches long or wide. If they're too small, you will take all day with this step in the process, if they are too large, it won't look as nice as it will with the right sizes.

3. Dampen your sponge brush, dip it in the decoupage glue and apply the glue only to where you are going to add the tissue paper. If you cover the whole votive now, it will dry or get tacky before you can lay down all the tissue papers and that will become frustrating for you. So take your brush and brush about a quarter of the space around the votive. From top to underneath. Then start to lay down pieces of tissue paper. Wrinkles are fine, overlapping is fine.   And trust me, it's ok for this to look like a mess right now. Wrinkles will add to the beauty of these.

4. Turn the votive upside-down and place it on the waxed paper to dry. This should take about a half an hour to dry completely. I have 6 stairs where I want to place these votives. I will be doing six of these. How many of these will you need? Make sure you have them all set out before you.

5. Let's take that nail file and go all around the rim of the votive to remove the excess paper that is hanging over the top. This doesn't take long and as long as your project is dry, you won't harm your work at all

6. Once your votives are dry, you will want to add another coat of deco glue to them. You will notice all of the wrinkles and may possibly even wonder how this is going to look when you are through. But keep the faith! You saw my finished product, and yours is going to look just as finished. When you add the extra coats of deco glue, like nail polish, it is best to add a light coat - don't glob it on-but add light (faster drying) coats each time.

Although about 4 coats should do these votives well, you can also go with 3 coats. I've actually been able to protect these glass votives by adding more coats of the decoupage glue on them. Our dog Angus knocked one down while running up the stairs and I held my breath as I watched it roll from the top step to the floor. None of it fell apart. There were actually a couple of cracks in the glass votive but the glue held it all together, and the cracks are not noticeable.

7. Once all of your pieces are dry, let's take a fresh new dry sponge brush and dip it in a topcoat. With humidity or heat, decoupage glue (even after it has dried) can become tacky. It's been my experience that even the decoupage glues that say "no top coat needed" right on the label, still need a topcoat. Always protect your pieces with a topcoat. And decide if you would like a glossy topcoat, a satin coat or a flat one. Apply the topcoat. You can always spray this on too. I prefer to brush it on in this case but that's up to you. I would rather not go outside with all of these to spray them so I'll use the brush on method. I find I have more control with the brush too.

Do you want to stop here? Let these dry and see if they look nice to you the way they are.

Would you like to add some trinkets? You could also just add some glitter to the tops the way you would with a margarita glass. Dip the top in some glue or use your finger to put some white crafters glue along the top rim. Have some tiny glass beads or glitter in a small container and "rim" the votive top. Let dry. When you are finished you will place your votive on top of the sheet of felt. I personally use the felt that comes with an adhesive backing. It sticks right away and stay's on for as long as I've been using it.

Use a pen or pencil to make an outline of the base of the votive. It's best to have a color that matches or compliments your votive colors. You don't want the felt to be the thing that stands out on your piece. Cut out the circle you've just made and remove the paper backing to reveal the sticky side. Attach this side to the bottom of your votive. No drying time needed. It's ready to be placed where you want it.

I would like to add some trinkets to my piece so I will continue. Here is what you'll need to continue. I am going to use brown velvet ribbon. If you are a crafter you probably have a little bit of every kind of ribbon on hand.

- Ribbon
- Fabric scissors
- Cherry blossoms (I got these in the scrap book section of the craft store)
- Tiny silk roses
- Hot Glue gun
- Fabritaq™

1. I measured one inch down from the top of the votive and laid the top of my ribbon here, circling the votive. I cut the ribbon so that the two pieces were just touching. I didn't want it to over lap and cause a bulge, nor did I want a gap between the two pieces. I did use hot glue to attach this ribbon but you can use Fabritaq ™

2. Once this was glued tightly in place, I added the branch with the cherry blossoms to cover the cut in the ribbon. Even though these branches have a tacky back already, I wanted to insure that they would stay on. So I put tiny dabs of hot glue in certain places to secure the branch.

3. Once I was done with all of these, I put one of the small votives that come about a hundred to a bag-inside of the aluminum holders-in the votive, lit them and took some pictures.

It's very nice when someone comes over and they see the foyer lit up only with the lights of these elegant little candles. Since I also like shabby chic, I did make one votive in a different design with a different shaped votive. The round one in the center has a tiny silk rose on the front of it. The choice of the votive shapes is completely up to you. And now?

You can light your candles!

HYDRANGEA BASKET

You can use any theme you want, I am using Hydrangea's because they are my favorite flower. I found these lovely napkins and had this basket sitting around for a while now. Ever do that? Buy something for some reason and a year later you find it still sitting in that same place? You're sure you'll remember what you got it for, so you don't throw it away. Besides, it's nice, unused and you paid for it. I also know that the day I give it away is the day before I find the perfect use for it.

This is where the organizational part of this book may come in handy. Can you use this basket to store an extra role of toilet paper in your bathroom? Or as a place to keep complimentary colored hand towels and soaps? What about as a planter? You can buy a plant liner-add some good soil and your favorite plant. Have you wanted to put your kitties toys away but really don't have a place?

Those are just a few of my ideas, but you probably have some of your own. I used mine in the bathroom; I rolled complimentary colored washcloths up and stored them within hands reach for anyone who takes a bath. This project is not difficult. There is no intricate cutting involved. Here is what we'll need:

- Small jar of decoupage glue
- Basket
- Decorative Napkins of your choice
- Spray bottle of water (with the finest mist you can find-craft stores and dollar stores carry these if you don't have any).
- Nail files (medium grit)
- Sponge Brush
- Glitter (optional)
- Ribbon to match your napkins (or twine)
- Waxed paper to work on
- A lazy Susan

Before you do anything--

1. Tear the hard edges off of your napkin.Go around the whole outside of the napkin and tear (do not cut) the hard edges off. We want soft edges that will disappear. Hard edges show through and don't look natural.

2. Peel away a layer of your napkin. Some napkins have 3 layers of paper and some only have two.   If it is three layers thick you will want to remove the bottom white layer before you get your hands wet or gluey. If you use all three layers the project will look lumpy and not as sheer as the look we are going for. IF you only use one layer, the paper is too fine and too sheer. It will tear too easily and the end result is not worth it. For this project it will be best to use two layers.

   On my basket I will need 4 napkins but I'll separate 5 just to be on the safe side. Take your napkins and place them around your basket to see how many you may need. It never hurts to have extra on hand especially when you are just starting with the art of decoupage. Mistakes happen but since these napkins are relatively inexpensive, you don't have to worry about it. You can dampen your thumb and index fingers and just put the corner of the napkin between them- rub lightly back and forth. You'll see the napkin starting to separate. Then just peel away the unwanted layer and discard it.

3. PLACE your basket on a lazy Susan. You may want to secure the lazy Susan so it moves only when you want it to. Dip a damp sponge brush

in deco glue. Get about half the brush covered in the glue. Put the glue down on the basket only where you will be working right now. In other words, don't coat the whole basket, just the small portion where you will be laying the napkins. Make sure that you push the brush into all of the grooves in the basket, so that you are not just coating the surface, but also coating the inside of the grooves.

4. LAY the napkin over the area you just brushed the glue onto. Since this paper is very delicate you will want to be careful not to touch it too much with your fingers. So attempt to lay it over the basket correctly the first time. No worries if you don't though, you have extras. Over lap the top of the basket making sure you have some extra napkin hanging loosely over the edge on the inside. The excess left over on top will be filed away when it's dry. You do want to over lap the napkins completely over the bottom edge. We want to cover the whole bottom with the napkins too. (The wrinkles that you will see are part of the project. The end result will be more of a dreamy and unclear image, yet like watercolor, it will work.)

5. SPRAY a fine mist of water over the napkin causing it to sink into the grooves. If there is an air bubble you can spray that tiny area again but right now I would not attempt to touch any of the napkin. It's that fragile. But the weight of the water will cause the napkin to sink into the weave, so you shouldn't have to touch it. You will want to wrap the napkin around the corners of the basket.

   *If you tore a little piece-you can cut out a tiny matching piece from your spare napkins and lay it over the hole. It will not stand out when it is dry.

6. REPEAT all of the above steps around all four sides of the basket. If you have any open areas on the bottom of the basket, tear a small enough piece of napkin to fill it in without wrapping it up around the outside of the basket.

7. DRY. You may find that the first side of the basket that you worked on is already dry. If this is the case, add another coat of the decoupage glue making sure to get into all the grooves now. The napkin will have been reinforced from the glue underneath it so it is sturdy enough to handle this coat of decoupage medium.   Just in case it still feels tacky, put it near a heater, or a sunny window to let it dry for at least 15 minutes. Make yourself a cup of tea, or if you're like me-treat yourself

to a Latte.

8. THOROUGHLY dry the whole piece now. You may want to leave it while you do some laundry-the dishes, or walk your dog.

9. ADD more deco glue to bottom and all sides of the basket. While it is still wet follow the next step if you are adding glitter.

10. TOP COAT. Take a fresh clean dry unused sponge brush and dip it in your topcoat. Since the topcoat can make a huge difference, you will want to choose this wisely. You can experiment with any old piece of wood, deco the napkin to it, let it dry and add the topcoat so you can see just how glossy or flat a finish is. Add the glitter while the topcoat is still wet. I would just do a light dusting so you can barely see it. In certain lights it will still catch someone's eye. This step is optional though, if you are going for a vintage look you may not want the glitter and you will want to stick to a flat finish.

    This next step is also optional. If you like the way your piece looks now, then leave it be. If you feel that it needs something else, add some ribbon or raffia.

11. ADD Ribbon or twine around the top of your basket. I once made an Easter basket following these instructions. I took twine and braided it like hair. I then hot glued the braided twine all around the rim of my basket and it gave it a lovely country feel that looked like something from nature. You may find a cute ribbon that matches one of the colors in your basket. If you have any excess napkin overlapping the top you can now simply tear it off and file it away with a nail file. Ribbon twine or pearls will cover any uneven pieces of napkin so you'll be safe.

12. Fill your basket! If it is to be used as a gift basket try adding items for a night of pampering. Pretty little girly flip-flops, feminine soaps, pastel colored washcloths, nail files, liquid soap and moisturizer. For fun, add some bubbles. Bubbles are fun for all ages!

My favorite idea about this gift is that one can reuse the basket once the gifts have been enjoyed. You will enjoy the feeling you get when you take the time to make a gift for someone with your own hands.

OCEAN FLOWERS JAR

Ever have one of these jars that are pretty, but you just aren't sure what to do with? Maybe that's just me because I am always looking for new ways to decorate things. I have a very hard time throwing pretty glass bottles and jars away. With the summer coming up I wanted to add a touch of the beach around our house.

Before you begin do a dry run before gluing any papers into place. Cut out your images first, and apply them to the inside of the jar you will be working on using a low tack tape. I usually end up rearranging the items a few times before I am satisfied with the pattern. This process is called Reverse Decoupage.

Here is our supply list:

- A pretty or unusual glass jar.
- Decoupage glue (available in craft stores)
- 1 inch foam brushes /several Low tack painters tape (available in hardware store and craft store)
- Sea sponges (available in craft stores and some hardware stores)
- Images from wrapping paper
- Acrylic paints to match or compliment your image
- Iridescent paint (optional)
- Blue Interference paint/ both of these paints add to the water effect.
- A shallow pan for water (old Styrofoam containers from meat are perfect for this and for use as pallets to place your paints on.)
- A lint free rag or cloth
- A toothbrush designated just for crafting. Flexible head works best.
- Zinsser™ stain cover spray paint. In hardware stores. *the one with the Red label

And, here are the steps.

1. Gather the acrylic paint colors that either match or compliment your project along with all other supplies.

2. Add only embellishments now-like vines or curly Q's with a liner brush. (This step is optional. If you are a beginner you may feel safer skipping this step.) I used a liner paintbrush and took some iridescent paint to make a few designs along the inside of the jar. This paint will dry quickly. (About 15 minutes) Touch it with your fingertip lightly to see if it's dry.

3. Dip your cut out flower/image in the water. Submerge the whole piece. Take it out and dab it on your lint free cloth.

4. With a foam brush add decoupage glue only to the inside section of the jar where you will be placing your item. In other words do not put glue all over the inside of the piece, just in the one area where you will be placing your image.

5. Place the image with the picture facing *outwards* on the *inside* of the jar.

6. Hold the jar up to the light. You will be able to see if there are any air

bubbles. Since the image is wet, you will now be able to smooth the piece out. This process is very messy, and it will certainly look it. Don't worry, because the glue will dry clear. Use your fingers to smooth out any air bubbles. You can also use a pop-sickle stick.

7. Brush decoupage glue over where you just placed your image now making sure it is completely flat against the glass with no air bubbles.

8. Repeat the above steps on all sides of the jar. (Inside)

9. Dry - let all sides dry. This can take about 15 minutes once you are finished applying your last image. You may have a heavy hand (like I do) and your piece may take longer to dry. Just touch it to see if it's dry.

10. Interference paint. I am going to use a very well wrung out sea sponge to apply the interference blue paint. Sponge the color all over sporadically. The purpose is to accent the piece; you don't need to cover every spot available on the jar. You can go heavier in some areas and lighter in others. This gives a nice effect. I am using a blue color, which is slightly shimmery, because it will *interfere* with the color of the green paint I will be using to keep in line with the ocean theme. Blue/green. Let this step dry thoroughly. This paint is very sheer and takes a short amount of time to dry.

11. Next splatter paint with a toothbrush around the inside. You can use a sheer color, or acrylic. The spatters will leave all types of different patterns and that is what we want it to do.

12. Have patience. Your piece may look like a mess right now. You may be wondering how this could ever turn out looking nice. I get to this point in almost every piece I work on. And it's rare that I don't genuinely feel proud of the work I've finished.

13. Dry. Give the piece about 15 minutes to dry. Is it time for a latte yet?

14. Sponge paint. Use at least two colors and for this project lets stick with blue and green so that we continue with the water effect. When sponge painting, you don't need to wait for the paint to dry between coats. They tend to blend and have a nicer appeal for this project.

15. Once your sponge painting is done, let it dry. (we spend a lot of time

drying don't we?) I would leave the jar near an air conditioning vent or a heater vent since that will tend to be the driest place in the house.

16. I let the piece dry over night and then used Zinser™ cover stain on the *inside* of the jar. This coat should be applied liberally. I took my jar outside and really made sure I got every spot covered. Leave the lid off the piece so that it can dry out for a few days. This white spray paint will serve two purposes. It will seal all of the paint and decoupage glue and it will cover up any tiny spots that you may have missed with the sponge. This paint will give the product a more cohesive look. And now you have a lovely container!

SMALL FOUND TABLE

For me, finding something that's being discarded, that I both like and can do something with is like finding a little treasure. I used to bring home all stray furniture knowing I could do *something* with it. My husband finally asked me to stop bringing home all of these items so that we could actually use our garage for the car. A very reasonable request, I thought. I could have opened a second hand furniture store but... focus.

In this project we are going to get into the act of cutting something out. I already have an idea in mind for this table. You may have a table, a chair, even one of those wooden cigar boxes. You can follow these instructions for those items too. Any wooden piece of furniture.

When I found this table it was all black and had a golden eagle on it. It was very traditional and Americana but not my taste.(I had taken pictures of that but that was two hard drives ago before I had learned about the importance of backing up my computer in case one's hard drive crashes…. Twice.)

There will also be some instructions on decorative painting, but no they're very easy to do.

The reason I am using two different yet similar colors on this piece is because this is an older piece with flaws in the wood. With one smooth coat of paint you would most likely see the flaws. But by using two similar colors of paint, with sea sponges I can easily camouflage it.

And by the way, you can use a piece of wax paper to experiment on when trying to figure out which colors will look best. A white paper plate works well for experimentation also.

If you need ideas on what to decoupage, think of what you love. Are you a beach person? Do you love shells and seagulls and Lighthouses? Or do you love flowers, leaves and trees? Maybe you like Victorian dresses. You can take pictures from magazines, books or greeting cards. Just make sure you make laser copies. Do not use your ink jet prints. Ink jet prints will run and smear when wet. But if you go to a copy store you can use the color printer to make lovely copies to use in your work.

Supplies

- Pictures or images you will be decoupaging (make extra laser copies)
- Heavy grit sand paper
- Disposable Plate or anything you can use for a palette for your paint.
- Automotive wet/dry Sandpaper (available in auto supply stores)
- 2 similar shades of acrylic paints (needed for imperfect surfaces)
- Decoupage scissors
- Regular scissors
- Decoupage glue
- Sponge brushes (available in craft stores and hardware stores)
- Brayer (small hard rubber brayer or an old credit card)
- Shallow water bowl (large enough for you to fit your image into)
- White Gesso (Excellent base coat)
- Clear Top Coat (spray or paint on is fine) gloss, satin or flat finish
- Lint Free dry cloth (I use a lint free window cleaning cloth)
- Lint Free damp cloth

Optional:

* Clear Wood primer if your piece is going outside. (available in craft store near acrylic paints)
* Stencil pouncing brushes
* Letter stencils or stamps
* Darker color of acrylic paint to stencil letters

1. Sand the whole piece using the heavy-duty sandpaper.   The purpose isn't to remove the old paint but we do want to get any loose paint or bumps off the surface. When you're done with sanding you'll want to use a damp lint free cloth to wipe away any residue.

2. Use Gesso to paint the whole piece. You may need two coats but probably not. You are still going to paint over the gesso so you don't have to be concerned if you haven't completely blocked out the old paint. The Gesso gives your piece a smoother surface and it hides any dark color that may be underneath. It's thicker than acrylic paint and has a chalky feel to it. Yet it dries smooth.

3. Dampen a sea sponge and wring it out so that it's almost dry. Pour a small amount of the *darker color* acrylic paint on a paper plate. Dab the sponge in paint lightly, then pounce it all over your surface. Cover most of the surface but not all. You want to be able to see some spots of the paint below (the gesso you applied) still showing through. Keep adding more paint to your sponge as needed. When you are done applying the first color, pour some of the second color of paint that you have onto the paper plate. Turn the sponge around and dip it in the second color and begin to apply it all over your surface. Cover all the bare spots and go over a lot of the areas you covered before. When you are done the colors will have blended yet have a stony look to them. Perfect for adding depth behind your images. If you're doing a beach theme you may want to use two colors that are similar in color to sand on the beach. If you're using flowers, you may want to go with a nature inspired color behind these.

4. Cut out your images while your piece is drying.   Although cutting sounds simple enough and it is…. there are a few area's that you may need help in. And here's one, when you are cutting an item that has an opening or a space that you need to cut out - like the handle in this tea cup you can go ahead and cut through the handle. You are going to be gluing (decoupaging it) back together anyway.

5. 5. Do a dry run. You will want to place your images down first without any decoupage glue. You will want to see what pattern looks best to your eye. Since you have cut out your images- lay them down on your surface the way you think they will look nice. Keep placing them in different places until you think they look good. You can also buy a very low tack tape (usually blue in color) from the hardware store and tape the pieces down so you can step back and take a good look at where you placed your images.

6. Decoupage. Take a sponge brush and dip it in decoupage glue. Apply the glue to the one section of the table or surface *only* where you will be applying your image. Dip your image into the water. Make sure it goes under the water; it's fine to get it all wet. (This is why I suggest everything get's copied at a copy center unless you have a laser printer.) Take your image out and place it briefly on your dry lint free cloth so that it's not runny or dripping. Then place it image side up, on your table over where you just placed the decoupage glue. If it's not quite right, if it's off center or not quite perfect, you can pick it up and re-position it a few times. That's yet another reason to dip it in the water first. Wet paper is far more pliable and easy to work with. Take your brayer. Roll it over the image several times so that you can see there are no air bubbles in the piece. If using an old credit card, just make sure you don't press too hard since it can tear your image. The idea is that you want to make sure you remove all air bubbles and excess decoupage glue from beneath the image. When you have finished with that image, wipe your brayer off with the damp lint free cloth to make sure it doesn't get sticky. I learned this the hard way. I didn't clean off the brayer, and ran it over the second piece I had put down and it started to pull some of the image away. Repeat this step with all of your images. If you have area's like I did on the leg of this table, that have grooves, you will want to use your wet fingers to move the images into the grooves.

7. When you are happy with the way your piece looks, you will now want to cover the whole surface in decoupage glue. Use your sponge brush and put decoupage glue all over. You can put it on just like you are painting. Making sure to go over all of your images. Let this all dry. This is the time I'll go make my Latte, do a load of laundry and take our dogs outside. It's best to give this about a half hour drying time. I always find something to do in this half an hour. Clean out that junk drawer. Go through that pile of papers and mail that just keeps piling up or just make my latte. I spend a lot of time waiting for things

to dry.

8. I am now going to apply my letters. If you don't want to do this step go ahead and skip to the next step. I know there are stencil paints out there but I would suggest using acrylic paints this time so that the drying time is equal to the other drying times. The pots of stencil paints are oil based and they take days to cure. I'm going to take a dinner plate, and place it in the center of the table. I'll trace (very lightly) around the plate, so that I know where to place the letters. You can make this circle so that it's only visible to you. Then as you stencil your letters on, you can erase the tiny bit of pencil mark left on your table. The acrylic paints can easily get under the stencils if they are too runny or wet. Make sure to blot your stencil brush before putting it over the stencil. Once done-Dry.

9. Put another layer of decoupage glue over your piece. Let it dry for an hour this time and sand it lightly with automotive grade sand paper. There are some decoupage professionals who will put between 10 and 20 coats of decoupage glue over a piece. This is to insure that the images raised surfaces don't show. It's always nice for people to ask, how did you do this? But I also know some people who are happy with a few coats of decoupage glue. I would use 5 minimum. Let dry between each coat. Under normal circumstances the coats don't take longer than a half an hour to dry. Once you're done with all the coats of glue, let dry.

10. If this item is going outdoors, you will want to put one coat of wood primer which is clear and is normally used to seal wood. The Primer will also protect your piece from fading because of UV rays. If this piece is going to be indoors you can now put a top coat on it. Do you want a high gloss? Satin or flat?

11. When your table is all done why not put it next to your lounge chair? Put a coaster down, along with your iced tea, your favorite magazine or book, and have a nice read while admiring the pretty work of art you've just created!

CUSTOM PICTURE GLASS BLOCK

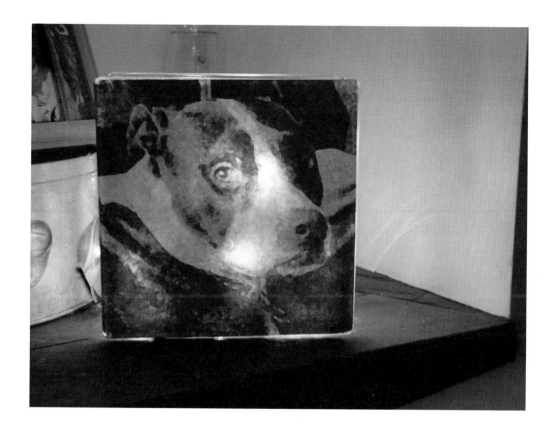

This is so easy to do you may get carried away with all of the pictures you love around your home. It's easy and a great personalized idea for a gift. The dog that you are looking at is my husband's best friend. My husband saw Angus while he was driving through a not so good area of a town near by. He's quite a handsome boy, and we had no intention of keeping him, but after a couple of month long fruitless searches for his owners, we adopted him. And fell in love with him. We already have enough pictures of him around the house, but maybe just this one more.

To begin you will need a laser copy of your favorite picture. You can make a copy first on your ink jet printer, then take this to your copy center where you can make a laser print on the self serve color copier. If you have a laser printer at home you're ahead of the game. The Glass Block that I purchased from one of the big box home stores measured 7.5 x 7.5. I printed out a full sized picture on the 8 X 10 setting, and just removed some of the excess so it would fit on the block.

Some glass blocks do have an opening at bottom in case you want to put lights in yours like I did. I was only able to find the glass blocks with openings in the bottom at Christmastime. I'm sure you can find them on line if not in other stores year round though.

- Decoupage glue Shallow bowl of water
- Sponge brushes available at hardware and craft stores
- Hard Rubber Brayer (You can use the back of a spoon but the brayer works best)
- Top Coat (preferably paint on as opposed to spray.)

1. COVER only the side of the glass block you are working on with decoupage glue using your sponge brush. Make sure to cover the whole area but don't glob the glue on.

2. DIP your photocopied picture in your shallow water tray.
   * Dipping the picture in water will make it easy to move around your surface.

3. PLACE your copy over the front of the glass block (If there is a hole on the bottom you'll want to decide if you want the hole to be on the top or the bottom. You'll want to be a little patient here. As you look down at the surface, center the copy. You will probably get very close to having it centered but find it is not quite perfect. Not to worry. This is why we got the copy wet. We can carefully move it around a little so that it is finally centered. You can over lap the edges if your copy is larger than your surface, or you can center your picture. If you do overlap the edges you can simply sand those off once the piece dries.

4. HOLD the glass block at an angle in very bright light. You will be able to see if there are any air bubbles that you would not see in normal light. And there will be.

5. BRAYER. Take your brayer and from the *center* of your piece, roll outwards towards all edges. (if you do not have a brayer you can use the back of a large spoon.) You will probably see glue seeping out around the edges. That's fine. You can remove that excess glue with your fingertips or a damp paper towel. Make sure that the edges of your image are pressed flat against the glass. Resist the urge to use your finger to get an air bubble out. A brayer is made just for this purpose and it's a nice smooth roll that won't interfere with the integrity of your work.

6. ADD more decoupage glue to the top of your piece. Keep it smooth.

7. DRY - this normally takes 15 minutes to half an hour depending on humidity. Once it is dry add one more coat of decoupage glue to the surface and let dry before adding your topcoat.

8. Top coat. So that you have more control I would suggest using paint on topcoat. The finish is up to you, gloss, flat or satin. And you're done!

You can now place tiny lights in the base-or hang a small LED candlelight down inside of your glass block. If you didn't get a glass block with any opening you can still place this piece near a window where sunlight will shine through it or place it in front of a candle

SCREEN or REFRIGERATOR MAGNETS

Have any holes or tears in your porch screen, your screen door? Or any screens in your house?   Or do you like to keep messages, photo's or invitations on your refrigerator? You'll love this simple fun project that makes so much sense. You can even change them easily depending on the season. Since you use decorative napkins it will be quite easy to purchase decorative napkins to match each season.   And here's a benefit of my having done this project before you. I tried to use magnets from the craft store. They were not strong enough to hold the thin wood cutouts. I looked on line and found something called Curiously Strong magnets. But I wanted them yesterday so I made some phone calls. I found out that Harbor Freight sells these very strong little magnets and so cheap!!! I bought 4 packs of ten. I have no need for 40 magnets, but I'll use them over the next several months. Probably. Since the magnets are so strong, you won't have to worry about items sliding off your fridge in the middle of the night.

Here's a list of supplies:

- Small thin wooden cut outs from the craft store. 2 pieces if using outdoors.
- Decoupage glue (Mod Podge is ok too)
- 2 sponge brushes (1 for decoupage glue and 1 for primer)
- Decorative Napkins or fabric (Napkins are much easier to use)
- Wood Primer (available in craft store near the acrylic paints-also available in hardware stores.
- Embossing powder (Ultra Thick Embossing powder works best)
- Clear embossing ink
- Heat gun (gets much hotter than a hairdryer.)
- Super strong Rare Earth Neodymium Magnets (from Harbor Freight) or curiously strong magnets available on line
- Waterproof topcoat
- E 6000 glue (available at craft and hardware stores)

* You learn something new everyday. As I was writing the instructions for this project we purchased a new trashcan that had a huge sticker right across the front of it that was not peeling off. My husband got the blow dryer and ran it back and forth over the label. It melted the glue and the sticker peeled off with no residue. Some of you may have already known this. But for those of you who find that some of those stickers leave a mess behind, there's a handy tip for you!

1. PRIME your wood with the wood primer from your craft store. Prime both sides. Dry. (Priming will weatherproof your piece. Rain, wind, cold, heat and humidity will take a toll on these if you don't prime them first.) If these are going to be used inside you don't need to prime them.

2. DECOUPAGE your napkin onto the wood by applying decoupage glue over the surface of the wood piece, then laying your napkin over top of it. Be very careful about smoothing out wrinkles. It's best to gently pull the napkin while laying it down to remove the wrinkles. There will still be some wrinkles. You do not need to separate the layers of the napkin but if you do, I've found that it works best to keep the one layer of white paper napkin still attached. Some napkins are 3 ply and some are only 2. The 2 ply makes it easier to decoupage. And it's less likely to tear when you are working with it.

3. Apply Decoupage glue only on one side of each wooden shape. One side of the magnet will face you and the other side will be seen by the world. If you are using these as refrigerator magnets, you will only need to decoupage one piece. Let dry.

4. SAND off the edges hanging over your piece. You can first tear off the loose edges but you will need to sand them also.

5. TOP COAT. Since this piece will be outside in the elements, you will want a waterproof topcoat. If you're using them inside any topcoat will do.

6. GLUE E 6000. Use this on the magnet to attach to the bare sides of your wooden pieces. Make sure you glue the magnets so they will attract each other and not repel. If you are making a refrigerator magnet you don't need to worry about this.

7. EMBOSS. Take the surface of your wood piece that has the image on it, and dab embossing ink all over it. You can find tubes of clear embossing ink refill or just use your clear embossing ink stamp pad. Make sure to cover the whole piece, and dip it in your embossing powder or pour embossing powder over it. Use your heat gun to melt the embossing powder. This part is fun!

8. DRY. Once your pieces are dry you can now put them on your screens or your refrigerator. Even if you don't have any holes in your screens, you can use them for decorative purposes. You can also just use them on your fridge for decoration or to hang little notes and reminders. Just think, these are so inexpensive and easy to do, you can do little hearts for Valentines day, Pumpkins or other shapes for Halloween, and naturally there are several different shapes out around Christmas and other holidays. You can always add some glitter to your wooden pieces too!

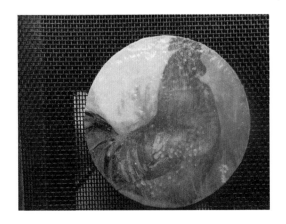

Pretty Tea Jar

We will be using a product that you will need to go to the hardware store to purchase. But there is nothing else like it. You will need it for this project and you can re use it in your home when needed. The product is called Zinsser Cover Stain. You can buy it in a spray or container. For our purposes, we'll use the spray. There are two different colored cans of Zinsser. One can is Red and the other is Gold. Purchase the can with the Gold label on it. This is an oil-based primer. Anytime you want to paint or decoupage on glass you will want to use this product. You can use your acrylic paints over this product even though you normally would not use an acrylic based paint over an oil-based paint. This product will need one hour to dry once you apply it. As long as you adhere to that guideline this will work. And you will not need to purchase special glass paints. Make sure to rub the glass with alcohol before spraying it with Zinsser™. It's only available in white as of this writing but it will always give your glass 'teeth' to grip the paints, papers and glues you'll be adding to it. When purchasing the paints for this product it is best to get them all at once so you can see if they compliment each other. Some pinks have a blue base, and some have a peach base. Ideally you will want to keep them all in the same color hue.

Here's what you'll need.

- Jar/glass air tight container (I used a glass Spaghetti Sauce jar)
- Zinsser® spray (in Gold Can)
- Spray paint for metal (Lid of jar) to match your projects colors
- Low Tack tape (available in hardware stores, craft stores and some supermarkets.
- Stencils , Stamps or 3 dimensional paint to print the word TEA on jar
- Laser Copies of Flowers
- Baby Pink Acrylic Paint –I am using 3 very similar shades of pink varying in intensity of color and these are not the actual names of the paint colors.
- Warm Pink Acrylic Paint
- Lightest shade of Pink acrylic paint
- Sponge brushes
- Sea Sponges (available in craft stores for painting)
- Decoupage glue (or Mod Podge)
- Rubbing Alcohol 91 % (available in the supermarket in aisle with pain killers.
- Decoupage scissors (available in any craft store and the kind that curve slightly are best for decoupage.
- Triple Thick High Gloss Top Coat in a jar though you can use the spray.
- Shallow water dish
- 400 grit sandpaper (automotive wet dry sandpaper)
- Lint Free cloth
- Glue E 6000 (available at Craft store-and it holds forever)
- Crystals (tiny ones are available on line or in the craft store, beading section.
- Ribbon with halved faux pearls on it. (I found these in the fabric/craft store)
- Piece of sticky back felt - available @ craft store for bottom of jar (optional)

Before we begin I will tell you that there will be a lot of drying time required between coats of decoupage glue. What I do is bring my project into the kitchen where I can return to it again and again as I do my housework, just to apply new coats of decoupage glue. You won't need to do this until after step 8.

Here are the steps for this project.

1. Once you have cleaned your jar, rub alcohol all over the outside of it. This works better (and is cheaper) than glass cleaner. And removes any oil that may be on the jar.

2. SPRAY Zinsser® all over the outside of your jar. (Do this outside) Always spray a light coat over the piece first. It is important to let this dry for one hour. One coat is fine; so make sure you cover all areas. Spray the lid spray with the metal spray paint.

3. Use your decoupage scissors to cut your images out while your base coat is drying.

4. PAINT your piece with acrylic paint once the Zinsser® has dried. You will find that using a textured painting technique will always add more appeal to your piece. And it will hide any mistakes that may have occurred with the base coat. I always spray too much in one area and it runs a little. The sponge painting along with the 3 similar colors of paint adds depth to what otherwise could be a flat looking piece. I use a sea sponge, but you may have some tricks of your own to use to make a textured background. Use whatever process you are comfortable with. (Practice on a piece of waxed paper first if you want to see how the texture and the colors will turn out.) When using a sea sponge, you will want to wet the sponge and wring it out so it's barely damp. Dip one side of your sea sponge in the darkest color of your acrylic paint first. Cover most of the jar but leave some spaces. Using a different side of the same sponge, dip it in the second darkest color while the first color is still wet. Dab the sponge over the rest of your jar, and finally with the same sponge, add your lightest and final color. You will see that not only will your whole surface be covered- there will be gradations of colors that have occurred. Set the piece near a heater or in the sun in a dry location for at least a half an hour.

5. Once your jar is dry you can start to place your images where you think they will look nice. You can lay the jar on its side and place a book on each side so that the jar doesn't roll. You are only doing a dry run to see where you will want to place your images permanently. If your piece is completely dry you can use a low tack tape. This is sold in hardware stores and some supermarkets and is usually blue in color. It would be sold near the electrical tape in the supermarket, not near the scotch tape in the stationery section of the store.

6. When you are happy with the look of your images decoupage them onto your jar. First, using your sponge brush apply decoupage glue to the area of the jar where you will be placing your image. Then dip your image in the shallow tray of water, take it out and dab it on the lint free cloth. Then carefully place your now pliable image down onto your jar over the decoupage glue. (If you have a lazy Susan you can put your jar on it instead of touching it as you try to move it around) Press your image down onto the jar and use your fingertip to smooth out any air bubbles. When getting air bubbles out always start from the center of the image and push the air bubbles out to the side. * One note of caution; be careful that you do not have any tacky or dried glue on your fingers. This can easily cause your image to tear.

7. DRY your piece. Let it sit for a good half hour in the driest environment possible. Go back and apply 7 to 10 more coats of decoupage glue. After the first 3 coats, sand with a wet 400 grit sand paper (the 400 grit may need to be purchased at an auto body store.) This is a very mild abrasive and is meant to remove tiny air born particles that have adhered to your jar. It will add to the final look of the product too. You will need to keep dipping the wet sandpaper in the water to remove what you have just sanded, then sand some more. When you are done, use your lint free cloth to wipe dry. Apply at least four more coats of decoupage glue over this drying between coats. When you are done with the last coat, let it dry for an hour. Sand it again with the wet 400- grit sandpaper. Remember to use your lint free cloth to wipe it dry when done. You will now want to leave your piece to dry for at least an hour. Put it in the most arid room in your home. (Outside if it's not humid)

8. Apply your stencil or stamp the word TEA on your jar. I wrote the word tea in pencil onto my jar. I then used 3- dimensional paint to write over it. Do whichever process makes you feel comfortable.

9. TOPCOAT I used a sponge brush and painted the Triple Thick topcoat on.

10. While the topcoat was drying, I added a thin line of E6000 glue all around the outside rim of the lid. I then cut my pearl ribbon and laid it over the glue. I then added tiny Swarovski crystals between the pearls.

11. This step is optional. Apply the felt bottom. You may want to do this if you have granite counter tops or any counter top to protect them from the glass jar being moved around. Simply place the jar over the sticky

back felt, trace the outline of the bottom of the jar onto the felt, cut out the shape, peel off the paper and stick it on.

You are now all set to put your tea bags inside of this. Naturally, you can store anything you want inside of it, sugar, sweeteners, coffee they will all stay fresh in a sealed glass container. To clean your completed jar, just use a damp lint free cloth. Do not put this in a dishwasher, or submerge it in water.

Chic Kitty Litter Box

Even if you don't own a cat, you can use this idea for that new kitten your friend just adopted. I think it's odd that as of today I cannot find a decorative Kitty litter box. Most kitty litter boxes are out in the open in most homes. Most are plain plastic. You can spend a whole lot of money on the lovely pieces that double as furniture)-but I would much rather keep the costs of things down.

And that's not the only reason I'm excited about this project. For one, no one else will have one-and I love it when someone asks me where in the world I got something. For another thing we all love our cats. And I felt pretty happy the whole time I was making this for my cats.

My husband's business is in a less than desirable part of a nearby town. There was a cat he thought was feral since she was running with other feral cats. But she used to go up to my husband to let him pet her. He always told me about this kitty and he said it was clear someone had dumped her. When it rained he would find her hiding underneath one of his long trailers out in his parking lot. She was too thin and was not wearing a collar. So my husband began to feed her. He commented that she was actually starting to gain weight. But a few weeks later he told me that oddly, she was only gaining weight in her belly. Since it was the month of

October I asked him to bring her home since the winter was coming and it sounded to me like she was pregnant. Thank God my husband is an animal lover too and he had bonded with Molly (she looked like a Molly to us). He brought her home. And two weeks later she gave birth to a kitten .The kitten was all black and I reasoned with my husband that we would have to keep this kitten since it was just the two of them and we had recently lost our 18 year old cat. The cats were taken to the vets, to be checked out. All was well, and we had our 2 cats and 2 dogs. (Until this past November when I brought home another stray cat that is now another member of our family and the most affectionate cat we've ever seen). I want them all to be happy. And even though they probably couldn't care less what box they piddle in, I like to think that I have given their bathroom a lovely home makeover.

A note before giving you the supply list:

When choosing a napkin pattern for your project, you will want to find a napkin pattern that can afford a few wrinkles. The beauty and challenge of working with napkins is that they will wrinkle. Small floral prints work well. Here is what you'll need:

- Spray paint <u>made specifically for plastic</u>, white or off white in color. Available in any hardware store or craft store. This is crucial to this project.
- Kitty Litter Box light in color (any plastic one you find in the pet store will work.
- Decorative Napkins
- Decoupage Scissors
- Decoupage Glue Or Mod Podge
- Sponge Brushes
- Top Coat
- Rubbing Alcohol (90 percent is best)
- Lint Free cloth
- Disposable cardboard box that is larger than the kitty litter box.
- Heavy grit nail file

1. Rub the outside of the litter box with the 90 percent alcohol. This removes any oils from the surface. You may want to wear gloves-since 90 percent alcohol can hurt your manicure.

2. Take the litter box outside and place it in a larger box-could be a box that you have left over from a shipment. Take your spray paint made especially for plastic and spray the inside of the litter box first and in 15 minutes you can spray the outside by just turning it upside down. Let dry. Spraying the litter box while it's inside of a larger box serves a dual purpose. You can spray the litter box and contain most of the spray particles so it doesn't fly around. And you can cover the box to prevent any dust from landing on the wet paint.

3. While the litter box is drying, open the napkin. Tear off all of the straight hard edges of all of the napkins you will be using. For a small kitty littler box use about 8 large napkins. You don't have to worry about separating the napkin layers for this project.

4. Place Decoupage glue down where you will be laying the first napkin piece. Make sure to spread some glue around the bottom of the box but only down to where the plastic seam is. Put glue on the seam too. Also spread some glue just under the lip on top of the kitty litter box. If you look at my picture you will see that the napkin is only decoupaged up to and under the lid.

5. Place the whole napkin down over the glue. Line up the torn edge of the napkin just under that lip on top. You should have some excess hanging beyond the seam on the bottom of the box. That's ok and you can just leave that for now.

6. Be careful as you place the napkin that you lay it down as flatly as you can - but at the same time, wrinkles are hard to avoid when working with napkins. Do *not* run your sponge brush over the top just yet. You will want to let the first coat dry. The napkins are so fragile that if you run the sponge over the top while they are wet from beneath you run the risk of tearing them and having to start all over.

7. Repeat this around the whole outside of box. Since the inside of the box will get a lot of scratching and it will be full of litter we aren't going to decoupage the inside.

8. Once the whole box has dried, you can now go around and tear away the excess napkin that you overlapped around the corners and the base. If needed you can use the nail file to sand away any papers that go beyond the seam.

9. Take a look at the box. Are there any tears? Blank spaces? Are there any spaces that just look like they need a little extra something? Go ahead and cut out a flower with the decoupage scissors. (Or whatever image is on your napkin) Add some decoupage glue to the box then place your image over it. Repeat this all around your box as needed. If you're happy with the way your box looks, you can skip this step.

10. Once the box has dried, you can now take your sponge brush to apply decoupage glue all over the whole outside of the box. You can probably see wrinkles when looking close up, but as you can see with the picture I have shown, you can't see them unless you are close up. Not too many people will get that close to your little box and it's unlikely that your cat(s) will mind the wrinkles.

11. Now apply 3 coats of decoupage glue. Letting each coat dry between. It normally takes about a half an hour for each coat to dry.

12. Add topcoat to the whole outside of the piece. I used a matte spray since I thought it would fare better over the long haul. I know my cats love their new box!

PLANTER/FLOWER POT

Here are the materials used for this project:

- Wrapping paper or wallpaper (find thinner images like flowers rather than pumpkins since they are easier to decoupage around the lip of the pot)
- Gold Flake
- Gold Flake Glue (both of these are available at your local craft store)
- Decoupage glue
- Sponge brushes

- Sea Sponges (or Faux sea sponges used for painting)
- Terra Cotta Pot
- Shallow dish of water
- Lint Free cloth
- Spray sealer for Terra Cotta Pots
- Gesso paint
- 2 Acrylic paints in colors to compliment your images.
- Top Coat -make sure you use an outdoor topcoat/sealer if this is going outside.

No matter what type of image or paper you chose to work with, you can follow these directions.

1. Spray your Pot with the sealer spray first. You will want to spray the inside and the outside. Let it dry. (You'll need good ventilation with this project) If you try to skip this step, your decoupaged planter will not last long. The images will get water underneath them and begin to curl up, fray and eventually fall off. It's not pretty.

2. While your sealer is drying you can cut out the images you will be using.

3. Once you have cut all of your images you can place them around the planter for practice. No glue, just a dry run to see where you'll want to place them. You may want to take a digital photo so you'll remember which image went where. Once you're happy with where you will be placing your images move to step 4.

4. Add one coat of Gesso on the outside only of your planter. Gesso dries quickly and works especially well on this surface. Let Dry.

5. Dip a slightly damp sea sponge into your darkest paint color and cover half of your planter with it. With a second sponge you will now pounce your second color all over your pot making sure to cover all of the spots where the gesso is. You can sponge on the second color while the first one is wet, or wait until it's dry. The two ending effects are different. The first wet on wet technique adds a much more blended appeal to the paint. If you wait until the first coat dries to add the second coat, you will be able to see a lot more texture. You can practice both of these techniques on a piece of copy paper first to see which one you would prefer. Once you are done painting both colors on let the piece dry thoroughly. I like₄₀

to put my drying objects near a heater or in a sunny spot inside of our home.

6. 6. You can now decoupage your images around the planter. Try to stagger them rather than just lining them up all along the bottom or top of the planter. You will notice that it can be hard to decoupage up over the wider part of the planter. The way around this is to make small cuts in the sides of your images right where they will be folding over that lip of the pot. This is why it's best to work with thinner or more narrow images.

7. Let Dry.

8. When completely dry you will want to take the glue used just for gold flake and place it around the planter where you will want to add the gold flake. You will want to overlap some area's of the image you have chosen, but not cover it. Same goes for the planter, you want to cover a lot of it, but not all of it.

9. Once your planter is dry, you can now add a topcoat. To keep the gold flake shiny I used a high gloss topcoat. And Viola!

You can present these planters at any time of the year as gifts. For a hostess gift you can roll up a dishtowel and a couple of kitchen utensils as long as they have nice stems to fit inside the planter. Put some clear wrap around it and tie it at the top, and you have a nice little something to bring into someone's new home.

For Christmas you can fill the planter with some glittery silk flowers, or just add a bouquet of candy canes. Decoupage the pots with Angels or Santa images. When someone isn't feeling well a lovely plant is always in order and imagine how much nicer it would be if you decorated it in the persons favorites color or images. Since you can find so many different shapes and sizes of Terra Cotta pots you can also make a lovely display for your own home. You chose the theme.

Romantic Rose Bucket

I liked doing this project so much. For one thing you can use metal containers that you may already have. Those large coffee tins work well for this. The very large metal containers you get at Christmas time with either cookies or popcorn in them. I use them for all types of storage but it's nice that they look like a decorative piece rather than some stuffy old plastic bin.

 I decided to work on a small metal bucket I got at the hardware store for less than 3 dollars. But these instructions work on any metal tin that you already have! Unless it's rusted. You would need to take the rust off and that would be a lot of time invested in an otherwise easy project.

I am using these romantic rose images that I've had for years. I simply made laser copies of them at the copy center and got to work.

I wanted to do this project to store extra rolls of toilet paper in. Once it was completed though I found a better use for it.I decided to put some sand in it, add some pearls, shells and beach glass. Then I added some votive candles.

I'm not writing this book to take you to new levels of decoupage skill. I want you to focus only on making something that you like and can reuse.

For this project I did a faux finish with acrylic paint on the surface of the bucket once it was base coated. It's very subtle and very easy.

Here's what we'll need to complete this project:

- Steel Wool pad Decoupage Glue Sponge brushes
- Sea Sponges (available in Craft store and some hardware stores)
- Decoupage scissors
- Wet/dry automotive grade sandpaper. (Grit 600) Available in auto supply stores and in some automotive departments of larger stores.
- Lint free cloth
- Small bucket from hardware store / Empty coffee tins work great too!
- Metal basecoat spray (This will prevent any rust/available in Hardware store)
- Acrylic paint in three similar colors to compliment your images
- Images of your choice
- Clean Styrofoam dish (or plastic paint palette)
- Shallow dish of water
- Paint on Top Coat water based.

1. Use a steel wool pad to scratch the outside surface of your can. Spray the metal base coat on the outside of your can.

2. Cut out your images while this is drying.

3. Once cans are dry, lay your images around the can to see how they will look before doing any gluing. You will want to make sure the images look appealing before you decoupage them.

4. Pour 3 colors of paint onto your Styrofoam dish. You don't have to be a master painter here but you do need to know a couple of rules when it comes to painting with more than one color. When working with acrylics you always want to use the darkest colors first and use the lightest colors last. You have to be careful with your color choices since sometimes the result of your painting can produce a "muddy" effect. That's why for this project I suggest you stick with just 3 similar colors.

5. Dip a damp sea sponge lightly into the darkest color. You don't want to cover the can. Since you will be adding more colors you'll want to only

add dabs of paint all around leaving bare spots for the other two colors. You can go heavier on any one color depending on the look you like. You don't have to wait until this step dries. You can rinse and squeeze the sponge you are working with and add your next color. Following the same instructions as with the first coat. Still leaving some of the white base coat to show through. When you are done with your second color you will then add the final color-again, while the previous coat is still damp. Dip it in the lightest paint and dab it all over the rest of the bucket, filling in area's that have no color.

6. Once your paints are all dry, place your images down on your tin can to see where they might look best before permanently gluing them. Some cans will have ridges in them, especially coffee cans and that's ok. The water you dip your images into will allow them to sink into the places it needs to. And with a gentle press from your fingertips, you can go around the can and make sure the paper sinks in.

7. When you are happy with the placement- apply decoupage glue to the area only where you will be putting your image.

8. Dip image in shallow dish of water and place it on your lint free cloth. This will absorb the excess water while leaving your image very pliable. Lay it flat over the surface. Take your sponge brush and place it in the center of the image smoothing the air bubbles out. Move your brush from the center of the image to the edge of the image. Flatten the image to the surface. Use a dampened finger to lightly push into any ridges that may be on the surface you are working on. Complete this step with all of your images until you are satisfied with how your surface looks.

9. Let all images dry. Add another coat of decoupage glue. Repeat this step at least 4 times and use a very fine auto grade sand paper once it's completely dry. The more layers of decoupage glue the more the image will look like it's part of the surface. Ideally, you don't want to see the edges of your images. It should blend in naturally like it's painted on. When I see a nice piece of decoupage work up closely I can see that it's got several coats of decoupage glue over it. The automotive grade sandpaper is very mild and perfect for taking out brush strokes and any dust that may have landed on your piece while you were working on it.

10. Once you are happy with the end result (and you may want to add another coat or two of decoupage glue, many professionals add 10 to

20 coats) you will then want to top coat your project. Flat topcoat means there should be no shine. Satin has a mild shine and gloss naturally would provide the highest shine. The paint on water-based top coats work very well with the acrylic paints and the decoupage glue.

You may have some good uses for this pretty little project too. As long as there aren't any sharp edges around the inside of the can you can use it near your laundry to keep your nylons and delicates in. Or keep it near the kitty litter box for disposable bags, or the scooper so it doesn't rest on the floor.

TISSUE BOX

This is perhaps the most used of all the items I have made. Everyone uses tissues. These blank wooden tissue boxes are available in a few places. The craft stores carry them. (In the unfinished wood aisle) Dollar stores tend to have porcelain tissue boxes. A lot of times they have designs on them already. But those are my favorite projects. Did you ever get a gift that just wasn't your style? I've taken porcelain tissue boxes that had a less than desirable theme on them, and turned those into styles that fit my home. Or I gifted someone else with colors or styles that I knew would fit their home décor.

For this project I am going to use the bare wood box from the craft store. If you are going to use a porcelain tissue box as your base, just use a coat or two of Zinsser™ on it before you do any work. Zinsser ™ is available at most hardware stores. The one in the red can is the one to use on glass or porcelain.

I used my own images and had them copied at the copy center. (Always make extra copies for those inevitable mistakes).

You may want to take pictures of your Children or a newly married couple. Would you like to see your pets or someone else's on the tissue box? You can use pictures of shells from the beach. What ever you would like to use to brighten a room. If these are going in the bedroom you may want a more relaxing image. Maybe you like to be surrounded by Angels. And for the kitchen, images of teacups. Coffee signs. Strawberries on the vine. And of course there are always the holidays. Seems tissues are in greater demand during the fall and winter holidays.

Here's what we'll need.

- 4 copies of a picture of a Sunflower including the stems and leaves. I went into my garden and pulled some Ivy along with the stems, copied it on my photocopier, made laser prints, and used that. I'm giving you a supply list of what I used (colors and images) but you can substitute whatever colors and images you would like. You can find these in books, on greeting cards or you can take your own pictures. You just have to make laser copies regardless of which source you use.
- Wooden Tissue box
- White Gesso
- Sponge brushes
- Dark Purple Acrylic paint
- 3 Dimensional paints (available in the craft store) to compliment your images. I chose a golden yellow color and a green for the leaves and vines.
- Decoupage glue
- Shallow dish of water (sterilized trays from your meat purchases work well)
- Hard brayer (the hard kind-not the one with a spongy roller)
- Lint Free cloth
- 600 grit wet/dry sand paper (Automotive grade-you may have to purchase at an automotive supply store.)
- Heavy grit nail file.
- Spray Topcoat

In order to find the perfect color for the background of this project, I took my sunflower image with me to the craft store. I held the image up to the purple tubes of paint to see which one best fit this project. I already knew that purple is on the opposite side of the color wheel from yellow. If you don't have a color wheel you can pick one up in the craft store for a few dollars. It not only comes in very handy for your craft projects but it also helps when decorating any room.

Here's how to complete this project.

1. Basecoat the outsides of the tissue box with Gesso. Make sure to cover the bottom too. (If you are using a porcelain tissue box you will need one coat of Zinsser spray instead of gesso.) Let Dry.

2. While the base coat is drying you can cut out your images.

3. With your sponge brush, paint the outside of the tissue box with your primary color. For me this was the purple color. Let Dry

4. While this is drying continue cutting. It's ok to cut the sunflower separate from the vine and leaves rather than attempting to cut one long continuous pattern. You will be piecing and gluing them back together anyway.

5. Do a dry run on where you want to place your images. For some interest I am going to wrap part of one sunflower over the top of the box. I'll also be continuing a vine around a side. Once you are satisfied with how you will place your items it's best to lay them out along side of your tissue box in the same order.

6. Brush decoupage glue on only the side of the box where you will be working.

7. Dip your image in the shallow dish of water, dab it on your lint free cloth and place it gently over the tissue box where you just placed your glue. Take the brayer and push any air bubbles or excess glue out. Roll the brayer outward from the center of the image. You may not see any air bubbles, or excess glue, but they are probably there. Don't skip this important step. Make sure to wipe your brayer clean of any excess glue or water as soon as you are done.

8. Pick up a piece of the vine now and place it along side the sunflower again using your brayer to smooth.

9. Continue with the leaves. Adding them onto the vine and if you would like folding them over the top or around the corner.

10. When you are happy with this side of the box, simply repeat these steps with the other three sides. And the top if you would like. Let Dry. Add four more coats of decoupage glue letting each coat dry in between applications. Usually a half an hour per coat will do it. Since we are outlining our images with the three dimensional paint, we do not need to worry as much about adding several coats of decoupage glue.

11. Take the 600-grit sandpaper to remove any impurities from the now dry surface. Wet the sand paper and gently rub around the whole surface. Don't worry, you wont' remove anything you have just done. You will however remove surface impurities that could take away from the smooth finished look of your project. Use a damp lint free cloth to wipe the whole surface when you are done.

12. Take your tissue box outside to spray it with your topcoat. Let Dry.

13. When project is completely dry, you can apply the three-dimensional paints. As a general rule, you want to use a matching color to bring out your images. For the sunflower you will want to use the yellow dimensional paint to outline the petals. Either outline the vines or add some curly-cues of your own. You may want to practice first on a piece of wax paper. Just to get the feel of how the dimensional paint flows.

14. When you are done, put this in a place where you can admire your work while it dries. The dimensional paint takes a little longer to dry than regular acrylic paint, but not much longer. You may start to feel very talented after this project.

15. When a day or two (in arid conditions) goes by, you will now want to top coat your piece one more time. The next time you catch a cold you'll have a little reason to smile when you reach for the tissues.

JEWELRY BOARD FROM AN OLD CABINET DOOR

Before we get started on this project I will tell you that you will need a drill for this. It's not as intimidating as you may think. I bought a small drill in the craft store that's perfect for me. I *was* using my husbands enormous and heavy man-tool drill. And what a difference this smaller lighter one makes. (You may feel more comfortable asking someone to drill a few holes for you too.)

That said, are you like me when it comes to your jewelry? I have a few boxes, which I use to toss my earrings into and one actual jewelry box. And then, there's my jewelry board.

This idea came from both a need and a want. I was decoupaging on cabinet doors. I got them from an auction web site but I can usually find them on sites like Freecycle or Craigslist. I've also had people call to tell me they were re-doing their kitchen and wanted to know if I wanted their old cabinet doors. More than once I've found them out in a front yard with a "Free" sign on them. For those of us who are considered creative types, these doors are blank canvases. And for a while I decoupaged the doors and hung them like you would a picture. But one day while going through my jewelry box, I was wondering how I could actually see some of the jewelry that I had purchased over the years. There were so many sparkly (Faux) jewels just hiding out in a dark box, I really wished I could have a better look at it.

Then I wanted to do something else. So I bought a couple of boxes of hooks and eyes from the hardware store. I did another decoupage project-but this time, when I was done, I simply screwed the hook eyes in strategically around the board. I say strategically because you'll want to be deliberate in your placement of the hook eyes. For me? I had a few longer necklaces, a few chokers, and a lot of dangling earrings. So I had to place the hardware in spots that I knew would prevent the jewelry from tangling.

Here's what we'll need for this project.

- A drill
- Cabinet door /available on line from auction sites/thrift stores or garage sales. Scrapbook papers
- Brayer
- Shallow bowl of water (I use disinfected Styrofoam meat containers)
- Lint Free cloth
- Damp rag
- Sponge brushes (3 or 4)
- * Water based antiquing medium that is also available in the craft paint aisle
- * Small container of water
- * We'll be mixing these in a baby food jar or other small container
- Gesso paint (white)
- 400-grit sandpaper
- Nail files that are normally used on acrylic fingernails (very course)
- Spackle (the premixed paste)
- Dust Mask
- Spackling knife (plastic or metal)
- Decoupage glue
- Top Coat
- Package of hook and eye screws (You only need the hook screw for this

project but I was having a hard time finding them without the eye screws with them.)

- Kit for hanging pictures (there are so many on the market that you may have your favorite. Video's are available on You Tube to instruct on how to hang.
- Decorative Ribbon or rope for hanging.

The first thing you will want to do is to decide what type of a theme you would like. Do you want a bold oriental theme in reds? Do you want a serene beach them in blues and greens? Just keep in mind that I am giving you instructions on making a vintage looking piece.

1. First, lightly sand the whole surface of the cabinet door using the 400 grit sand paper. Wipe it clean with a damp lint free cloth.

2. Paint the surface you will be working on with Gesso and let it dry. One coat is fine.

3. Tear your scrap paper instead of cutting it. I took scrap paper that had Hydrangeas on it and just tore the hydrangea's out. A nice tip for tearing is to take a tiny paintbrush like the kind they use in paint by number sets. Dip the tip in water and just like if you were using a pencil, draw an outline with water around the image. You'll have to keep dipping the brush in the water as you make the outline but you'll find it makes the tearing so much easier.

4. Lay the board flat and place images sporadically over it for your dry run. When you are happy with the pattern you have created, carefully remove your papers and place them down in the same order within reach of your hand alongside of your cabinet door.

5. Let's start to decoupage. Begin at the top of your piece and first dip your torn paper into a shallow dish of water, blot it on your dry lint free cloth. Put some decoupage glue on the back of the paper with a sponge brush. Don't glob the glue on but do make sure the whole piece has glue on it. Place it down and use the brayer from the center of the paper moving outwards in all directions to secure the piece.

6. You will repeat these steps for each piece of paper you want to put down.

7. Let this dry for at least a half an hour. Do you have laundry to sort or fold? A call to make? I've always got a list of things I need to get done

on stand by. You can now add your Spackle. This can be a lot of fun even if you've never worked with it before. Chances are you have never worked with it this way anyway. So let's get out our Spackle knife and start to swipe some over our project. Use your Spackle knife like a butter knife. Only instead of evenly spreading butter, you are going to deliberately leave some ridges and high points in your piece. And you will want to cover some of the edges of your papers. Keep stepping back to get an idea of where you want to add more Spackle. Keep in mind that you will be sanding down a lot of the areas where you have added it. So that you can see the image coming through the Spackle.

8. Let it dry. This dries surprisingly fast. You can usually begin to sand the first place you applied the Spackle just after you have finished applying it to the last place. Before we start to sand I would strongly recommend going outside. Even though you are going to wear a dust mask for this step, the dust particles are so fine; you are going to want them outside where they can disperse and blow away. I don't want this dust getting into my vacuum cleaner either.

9. I use a nail file because they are very flexible and the grit seems just right. As I file I want some areas to be filed right down to "almost not there" and some areas I want to stay raised-and appear to have cracks in it. You'll get the feel for this as you work.

10. Again, keep stepping back-take a look at your piece in strong light, sunlight if possible to see what you like and where you may want to do a little more work. Take a slightly damp rag and once you have blown all the dust particles away, use the rag to lightly wipe away the particles that are still clinging to the board.

11. Now mix equal parts of antiquing medium and water. Try one tablespoon of each. Stir it well. Take a sponge brush and apply it to one 8 by 8 inch area of your board. It does look dark going on but don't let that worry you. Once you've applied this solution, you are going to rub it off. Use your lint-free *damp* cloth. I know I ask you step back a lot but you really want to see this piece from a distance since it is a larger piece and you normally will be standing at a distance when you look at it.

So? Do you like it? Do you want to darken it? Lighten it? You can always do some more sanding if you want to lighten it, or repeat the process with your solution if you want to darken it. But do you notice where the solution has gone between the cracks of the Spackle? That's what we're going for. Apply this aging solution to the rest of your door. Let it dry.

12. You can now spray or brush on your topcoat. Let it dry.

13. You may know how to use a drill or you may need some help with this. But this is when we are going to put the hooks in. I used a pencil and a ruler to space the hooks evenly apart. You may want a lot more hooks than the amount that I used. You may not want to set the hooks so they are even. You may want to place them sporadically around your board. I am not a very mathematically inclined person but I did measure the width of my door, so that I could divide it by the amount of hooks I wanted to use. You can eye ball it if you want, or use a grid of some sort. Do what makes you feel comfortable.

14. Your piece is now done except for the ribbon or rope you will use to hang it. I simply hammered two nails in the back top corners of my door, attached a wire ribbon to the back of the piece. You can look on You Tube for videos on "how to hang a picture" too. You can now not only organize your jewelry but you'll be able to see it more often! This is the spackle over the hydrangea with the wash over it.

Repurposed Wine Bottle Mad Men Style

My friend has this amazing talent for decorating. You know those homes you walk into and somehow it looks like a showroom yet homey? There's a vibe to it, a feeling. It's got " the look". It all flows and works together. The colors and the textures, the placement of things. How she does it-I don't know. But I do know that she has a real eye for the vintage. She's not the type to buy something because it looks vintage, she will get it because it *is* vintage. So even though I am making her something that will look vintage, I am using newspaper ads from an actual 1945 Sunday Newspaper. The paper is old and tattered and would probably not be very resilient. So I have made copies, but not in black and white. I used the color copier in the copy store in order to keep that golden aged look to the paper. Even though technically this is still not vintage- I know she'll like it.

I'll also be using oil-based varnish instead of water based. These oil bases already have an aged tint to them. A warm subtle amber color. These are readily available at your local hardware store. You will need to pick up a spray can of Zinsser™ while you are there too-because we'll want to give the empty wine bottle a surface other than the glass to hold our designs. Here is a list of supplies of everything that we'll need.

- Exam gloves (available in any drug store) you want a tight fit. Tinted polyvinyl in small can. (Purchase two similar colored tints.) Stipple brushes (used just for the polyvinyl)

- This is a very good stipple brush I got from Dick Blick Art supplies on line. The brushes are often round but use whatever makes you comfortable.
- Oil paint clean up for brushes
- Empty Wine Bottle
- Lint Free cloth
- Bottle Pourer (available in Home stores & a lot of supermarkets.)
- Zinsser™ Oil Based Spray Paint-available in hardware stores, with the Red label.
- Vintage Images (if you can't find any vintage newspapers or magazines around- do a search on line for free vintage images. There are so many lovely ones that you can download on your printer. I always advise making a laser copy of your ink jet prints since ink jets will run with

water or solutions on top of them. Laser prints are waterproof.
- Decoupage scissors
- Decoupage Glue
- Sponge brushes
- Small cup of clean water
- Shallow tray for water
- Dishwashing soap (like Dawn)
- Baking Soda
- Drop Cloth
- Automotive sanding paper (wet/dry 1000 grit)

Since you will need to soak this bottle for a bit, and you will be spraying a couple of coats of Zinsser™ on this bottle, you will have some time to cut out your images.   It's always a very good idea to have at least two of the same image so that you have a spare piece in case the first one tears, or if you just don't like it and end up taking it off the bottle. When you're first starting out in decoupage a few things can go wrong. But don't let that worry you. I've been doing this for years and I still cut out a spare image and sometimes even another spare.

1. 1. To begin-we have to get the label off of the wine bottle. Normally this would be a challenge. Not to worry though. Here's the best way to handle it. The material around the neck of the bottle is usually not paper so you can just take a box cutter and run it down the side and easily tear this off. Fill a sink with the hottest water you can. Add soap and let the bottle sit-submerged for 15 minutes in the hot soapy water. (During this time you can cut out your images.) The label will come off on it's own, and anything left on the bottle can be easily peeled off. But there will be glue on the bottle. Take some baking soda and dishwasher soap and make a paste of it. Rub it into the glue on the bottle for a minute or two. Then rinse. Make sure the inside of the bottle is washed too. This works on all labels by the way. Jars, bottles etc.

2. You can hand dry the bottle with a dish towel then take it outside to spray a few lights coats of the Zinsser™ spray on the outside of it. Take about 15 to 20 minutes between coats depending on the humidity. It's best to use two light coats of Zinsser as opposed to one heavy coat. You can continue to cut some images while you are waiting for your bottle to dry. Don't worry that the images are going to look stark on the bottle. When we add the oil-based varnish, we are going to give the bottle some depth with the two colors of varnish.

3. Now that everything is dry, and the images are cut we are going to decoupage them onto the surface of the bottle.

    First, let's use a sponge brush to paint some decoupage glue onto the bottle surface just where we are going to place our image. Put some water in a shallow dish. Carefully dip your image into the shallow water. The idea is to get the whole piece of paper wet. This way, when you lay it down-the weight of the paper will flatten itself down to the bottle. Leaving you with less air bubbles and less wrinkles. It's also much easier to work the air bubbles and wrinkles out. Dipping my images in water made all the difference in making my decoupage look professional as opposed to when I was just starting out in decoupage. Please don't get discouraged if you tear any part of your work. Sometimes you can just push the torn pieces back together. You are working with glue anyway right? But one challenge you may find when working with bottles is the curve of the bottle. One of my images is a little taller than I had intended, and I had to slightly bend the head over the curve. I had to be careful not to wrinkle the face while smoothing out the paper. I know that if I smooth too much, I can rub away some of the paper, losing some of my image. Ideally, you want to handle your image as little as possible. Although I did have to lift my image a couple of times before I got it right. This is yet another reason to wet the image and make sure you have a spare on hand. Instead of the paper being dry and tacky - it is wet and fluid, allowing you to move it around more without lifting it. For the image of the smoking man, I simply lined the bottom piece of the image with the bottom line of the bottle. Make sure you hold your piece up to the light before it dries. You can easily see air bubbles that you may have missed before. If you find an air bubble, you can use a pin, prick the center of the hole and move the air out, or if the piece is still wet enough you can smooth the air bubble out to the nearest edge. You can (gently) use your damp finger to move this out.

4. Let the piece dry for at least a half an hour. Apply another coat of decoupage glue over the whole bottle, let dry for another 20 minutes. Have a heat vent you can place it near? Or a particularly dry or sunny room where the drying process can get a little help? Dry your piece in the most arid conditions possible.

5. After you have applied and dried 4 coats of decoupage glue, take your wet automotive sanding paper (make sure it is wet/dry sanding paper) to remove any air borne particles that may have attached themselves to the piece while drying. This will also smooth out any imperfections

that aren't *that* visible to the naked eye but make a difference in the end result. Remember that you are not sanding per se, rather gently going over the piece to smooth out any slight imperfections or dust particles. You should be dipping your sandpaper in and out of clean water to remove anything that you have collected while sanding.

6. When you are done, use a lint free dry cloth to remove any dust. Take your bottle outside or into a well-ventilated area. Bring your varnishes and stipple brush with you along with a box or drop cloth to work on. I have to admit that I always think that I can coat my piece inside in the basement where the fumes will not affect anyone. But there is not proper ventilation in there and I end up with either a headache or a sore throat from the fumes~ therefore I have learned that it is important to go outside to varnish. You probably already knew that, I sometimes learn the hard way. We are going to apply 3 coats of varnish to the piece.

7. Open your polyvinyl varnish starting with the darker tint first. Using your stipple brush, dip it into the varnish and blot it on a napkin (so it doesn't run) before applying it to your piece. These colors are sheer but we really only want to age the piece. So be careful not to overdo it. Sporadically pounce the brush all over the bottle perhaps using a pattern like the Milky Way. Clusters of stars that almost have a form or shape. Do not cover the whole bottle. I accented the curve of the bottle in one area, and then moved around the piece in an inexact manor. Nothing should be exact here. It should be fluid. This is why we're using a stipple brush. If the varnish is dripping or running down the side, you have used too much and only need to blot more. You can always wipe the varnish off while it's wet if you want to. You won't hurt the image now that it's under the decoupage glue. When you are happy with the first coat move onto the next color/hue of varnish and apply it the same way, it's best to do this before the first coat dries. When you are happy with the second coat you can go back to the first color of varnish and fill in all of the bare spots left on the bottle. You may wonder why you need to apply the first coat a second time. That's because you don't want to over do it in the beginning. This going back over the first and second coat helps give the piece a more cohesive look, more blended and naturally aged. Once you're finished applying the varnish you can set the bottle on a piece of waxed paper in a room that you can keep closed, Attic? Basement, spare room or garage. Leave it over night and when you wake up you'll be excited to go see the piece of functional art you created the day before!

Paper Mache Bull
From Vintage Poetry Book Pages

Where would I be without the internet? Thanks to it, I'm going to learn about this vintage paper I am using. And this *is* vintage. I bought this paperback book at a garage sale. The pages have browned so nicely and tearing it is quite easy. But what if the paper is so old that the varnish eats through it? Or eventually destroys it? I will do some research and find out what might work best when working with vintage paper.

OK, so after finding several new web pages to add to my favorites, I did come up with a lot of information about the varnish. Suffice it to say, it is safe to use it on vintage paper, however I also learned that 3 coats is the norm. For both protection and a deep finish. Since varnish does take longer to dry, (oil based) you will want to keep it inside of a larger box if possible so that air born dust won't fall onto your wet surface and stay there. There are several warm hues that go along with using an oil-based varnish. So we'll attempt to use the one with an amber hue because I know this will help make the piece look authentically older.

Here's what we need for this project.

- An old book
- A Paper Mache animal of your choice (available at craft stores)
- Decoupage glue
- Sponge brush
- Varnish (oil based) available now in craft stores as well as hardware stores.
- A sewing needle (no worries, not to sew)
- A shallow bowl of water
- A ribbon   (That will compliment your piece and decorate your Bull's neck.)

And here's how we do it.

1. To begin we'll want to tear out several pages from the book. If you're curious as to how many pages, it's always best to have too many so tear up a lot more than you think you will need. Obviously it will depend on the size of your piece. A good rule of thumb is to look at your paper Mache animal as if you were going to wrap it. How many pages would you need? Then you'll add about ten more pages to that.

   And make sure you tear off those hard exact straight edges. You will need some larger pieces of paper to cover the larger areas and smaller pieces to go around the curves of your paper Mache object. Tear some very small pieces too. You will need those to cover up some tiny spots when you're done adding all of the other pieces. Not much though. It's best to do this ahead of time since it's not the time to do it when your fingers are covered in decoupage glue.

   And I will tell you ahead of time- there will probably be wrinkles in the pages as you apply them, but that's really not a problem. It will all come together when you're finished.

2. Now that you have torn all the pages you can start to decoupage. Put the decoupage glue on a small area of the paper Mache item. This is where you will be placing your torn pages. Don't worry about being too neat or exact. You will want to overlap the pages. Dip your page pieces in the water, dab it on the lint free cloth and apply it over the decoupage glue. That needle that you have is for poking tiny holes into the paper where you can see there is an air bubble underneath. This usually happens under the larger pieces of paper that we've put down. This is also why you will first dip your paper into water. Best to smooth

it with your wet finger than the sponge brush. You can get a feel this way for the areas where you have to press the paper down into a gap. Basically you will just do these steps all over your bull. Use larger pieces of paper to start, and smaller ones to fill in the rounded or bumpy areas.

3. Apply 3 coats of decoupage glue, letting dry between each coat.

4. Apply a high Gloss varnish. Let dry.

5. Add a ribbon around your piece. Viola!

Decorative Water Pitcher

When I first bought this pitcher I knew it would be for decorative purposes. It was already decorated but images had faded and were not in my taste. I had it in my bathroom on the tile ledge on the side of the tub. As a few years went by,I could see the paper peeling away from the pitcher. All of the humidity in the bathroom was too much for it. I decided to immerse the whole pitcher in very hot soapy water and remove all of the paper. (And here I thought this had been hand painted.) You can start with a plain old metal watering can. Old or new.

First, here are the materials you'll need.

- Metal base coat (spray paint available in Hardware stores) Metal watering can (or pitcher)
- Steel wool
- Lint Free cloth
- Decoupage glue
- Decoupage scissors
- Sponge brushes
- Floral images
- Stick on letters (You can also emboss or stencil the letters)
- High gloss topcoat Shallow bowl water
- Spray paint (color of your choice to compliment your images) 90% alcohol (in the band aid aisle of your supermarket)
- Latex or surgical gloves
- Lint free cloth
- Lazy Susan (not crucial but it will make this project easier)

1. Decide first, what flowers you will be using on your pitcher. I was going for a springtime theme and had the flowers for the piece in mind when I selected the color of spray paint. You may want to do a fall theme, with leaves using oranges, rusts and yellows. You may want an ocean themed pitcher. Have your ideal finished product in mind.

2. Use the alcohol to wipe away any grease or oil that is on the outside of the watering can before you spray paint it. This is where you'll need the gloves. Protect your skin while taking this grease/oil off.

3. Rough up the surface with steel wool. Wipe the surface with the lint free cloth and shake it out once you're done. Best to do this outside.

4. Spray paint your piece first with the metal base coat. Dry.

5. Spray paint your piece with your colored spray paint. I used a very soft pink because I was going for a springtime theme.

6. While the spray paint is drying cut out your flowers or images. By the way, it's January in the Northeast so I wasn't about to spray paint this outside and leave it there. It would have frozen before it dried. I took a large box outside and placed the pitcher inside. I spray painted it lightly, brought the whole box inside and placed it inside an unused room to dry. I closed the door and left it there for about 20 minutes. I

then took it back outside and repeated another light coat-in the sun so I could see if there were spots that I missed. Then, I brought it inside and returned it to the spare room. With the dry heat blowing, it made for optimum drying conditions.

7. You will want to do a dry run with your images first to see where you would like them to sit permanently on your pitcher. You can use tiny pieces of low tack tape if you want. I just put books on each side of the pitcher to stop it from rolling or moving as I placed it on its side. I then just laid the flowers down where I thought they would look good. A good tip might be for you to take your largest image or the one with the boldest color and place that down first. This will be your focal point. Try to place it on an angle or move it just off center to either side. Or do both. Place all other images around that main piece.   When you are happy with the placement of your images, lay the pieces down next to you in the same order you will be decoupaging them in.

    Once you're happy with your layout you can began to decoupage.

8. 8. Place your pitcher on the lazy Susan. I place the two books on each side of the lazy Susan to secure it. You won't want it spinning or moving while you are trying to decoupage. Using your sponge brush place some decoupage glue on your pitcher only where you are going to apply your focal point piece, your first piece.

    Dip this piece in water and lay it on your lint free cloth to absorb the excess water. Then lay it over the area where you just applied your decoupage glue. Make sure you gently use your finger to push excess glue and/or water out to the nearest edge of your image. In other words, you wouldn't see an air bubble on the left hand side of your image and force it out all the way over on the right side. Instead you would place your finger or your brush in the center and move the air bubble out to the side. Continue to brush from the center of the image out spreading decoupage glue over the top of the image. One thing I am always thinking as I decoupage, make sure the edges are glued down firmly. Make sure you move the brush back and forth over the edge. The movement of the brush outward will push the edges down, and the movement of the brush back toward the center will fill in any microscopic holes under the image. While you keep repeating these steps a few times, you can feel better knowing that your edges will not come up. Basically, you will just finish this process with all of your images until you feel you are happy with the way your pitcher now looks.

9. I am using stick on letters. The letters are precut with adhesive already on the back of them. I obviously will not need to use decoupage glue on the backs of the letters. Since they already have glue on them, I am going to just place them where I see fit. I *will* however still put decoupage glue over the top of them and secure them in the same manner. You still don't want any loose edges. If you would prefer, you can emboss your pitcher. Or use stamps.

10. Once your pitcher has dried, you will want to add at least four coats of decoupage glue to the piece. More coats are always better but you will need to use the automotive wet/dry sand paper between coats, and you will need to dry between coats. Once all the coats are dry, let the piece sit for a few hours.

11. You can now add the varnish. The varnish I am using requires only one or two coats. This was purchased in the art department of the craft store. Please make sure to use a fresh brush when applying the varnish. I've tried to cut corners in the past using the same brush that I decoupaged with. And I've either had some cloudy results or bits of debris had collected on the brush, even after I had rinsed it thoroughly. Let the varnish dry and this is now ready to be used to hold flowers, or since we didn't work on the inside, you can actually water flowers with it!

CONTEMPORARY KOI VOTIVE HOLDER

Every once in a while I want to move away from my romantic roots and make something that looks contemporary. I saw a greeting card that was the basis for this project in an art store and knew I wanted to make something of it. I had this rectangular glass vase in storage. (Where it was never lonely.)   I think I used it once to put stones and twigs in. I knew that one day I would want to use the vase for decoupage purposes-and here's that day.

Here's what I used.

- Decoupage glue
- Decoupage scissors
- Copies of Koi fish
- 91 percent rubbing alcohol
- Shallow dish of water
- Light Blue tissue paper * the tissue paper that you include in gift bags)
- Light Green tissue paper
- Small flat edge paintbrush (similar to what you would use in paint by number)
- Glitter (optional)

- Rectangular glass vase
- Ultra high gloss topcoat (A good one is called Triple Thick)
- Lazy Susan (this makes it easier to work but you don't have to have it.)
- Fine Mister of water

With this project we'll be working on the outside of the glass.

Sometimes when working on the inside of glass the very high gloss of it will hide some of your work since you can only see the glare and not all of your art work. So we'll work on the outside.

1. First rub the alcohol all over the outside of the glass.

2. Tear up enough pieces of the tissue paper to cover your vase. Since you will be covering the whole outside you can just wrap a half a piece of each color around it to see if it covers it all. This way you will have more than enough. And you'll want to tear off the hard straight edges. We don't want any hard edges.

3. Place your vase upside down on your lazy Susan or surface of your work area. There are a few tricks to working with tissue paper. It is so very fine that you may get frustrated if you tear it or it bunches up on you. But here's how to avoid that. Keep your paintbrush wet all the time. Keep your fine mist spray bottle near you so you can also spritz the paper along the way to help it lay flatter. Step by step here is how you will lay down one piece of tissue paper. Place enough decoupage glue down on the glass where you will be laying the paper down. You don't want the layer of glue too thin or too thick- just don't be heavy handed with the glue. Lay the tissue paper down horizontally. And gently pull the paper so that it's flat as opposed to bunched or wrinkled. You might find this a little challenging. The worst that will happen is the paper will tear and you'll simply remove it and use another piece. Nothing to feel stressed about. I mention this because

when I make beginner mistakes I tend to have a knee jerk reaction. And that reaction is, "I'm not good at this." Obviously I push through that but I did have to learn to tone down my inner critic.

You may notice a few wrinkles and that's ok although we are trying to Avoid those in this project.

4. Use your flat brush to place some decoupage glue over the piece you just laid down. * This is important...Always keep your brush moving in one direction with this project. If you go back and forth with the brush, the paper will easily come loose, bunch up or tear. And *that* will frustrate you. For the bottom of the piece you will want to tear the edges of the tissue paper so that it does not over lap and go up the sides. When you are satisfied with the bottom you will let it dry for a good hour. If you have the heat on, you can place it over a vent and begin to work on it again in a half an hour. If it's not the season for you to have your heat on, you can just put it in the driest room in your home. While the piece is drying on the bottom you can now cut out your pictures.

5. Repeat all of the above steps to complete covering the vase with the tissue paper. You *will* want to overlap the paper around the bottom of the vase. The tissue paper easily folds over the edge where you can tear some excess or fold it around the corners like you are wrapping a gift.

   Once the whole vase is covered give it about a half an hour to dry. You'll know it's dry when it's not tacky to the touch. Here's what your vase should look like now.

6. When the piece dries you may notice that you missed a spot or two. Always take your piece near a sunny window or at least, the brightest light you can find. Look at it in the harsh light. Just add pieces of the tissue paper where you need to. You may also notice that there are few places where there are lumps or the paper bunched up a bit. You can use a strong cardboard nail file to file these lumps away. If you hit bare glass, No problem-just add some more tissue paper there. Let it dry for about 15 minutes.

7. Do a dry run with your images. Lay your images down to make sure

you like the lay out. Sometimes, this is the roughest part of a project for me. I'll put flowers down in a pattern; let's say I will use a diagonal pattern. But I'll step back and look at it and think, "hmm".... Something doesn't look appealing to me. I'll rearrange the pieces and it still won't look good. I have to admit; there are times when I will go on line or through some of my decoupage books for inspiration. If you don't have any other decoupage books on hand, you can always go to Google, type in decoupage, find something that inspires you. A design. You will see so many things pop up that you will soon have several ideas on how to lay your images out.

8. Once you are happy with where you will be placing your images, Decoupage them. Add a light coat of decoupage glue to the back of your image using your sponge brush Using the same brush apply a light coat of decoupage glue over the top of the image. Use your fingertip to press the image firmly down making sure there are no air bubbles underneath. Apply the rest of the images around your vase. When you're done applying your images apply a coat of decoupage glue around the whole piece. Let dry for an hour.

9. Repeat this until you have at least 4 coats of decoupage glue on your vase. Let the piece dry for 15 to 20 minutes between each coat. After all coats of decoupage glue have been applied give it an hour to dry.

10. I wanted to add a very light dusting of glitter to make my piece have more of a watery effect. If you would like to add glitter, use a sponge brush to paint your topcoat on. While it's still wet, sprinkle a tiny coating of glitter over the surface.

I'm very happy with the piece and the soft glow this emits.

BEACH TILE COASTERS
FROM BATHROOM TILES

Today we are experiencing an ice storm. Yes, we're getting it all this winter. Blizzards, snow storms, Nor'easter's, and sleet.   It will turn out to be not as bad as it was predicted, but it was bad enough to keep me indoors.

The Saturday night prior to the ice storm we had gone to our neighbor's house for dinner. They had another couple over who lived nearby and we all had a lovely evening. But as the men all gathered around the island talking about golf, the women were near the cozy fire sitting in a nice deep couch. I noticed a shortage of coasters for our drinks. I began to visualize what I would be making for this couple.   I didn't want anything too feminine, especially since coasters tend to go in the family room. I was trying to come up with a neutral theme.

But as we all talked about the ice storm we also talked about how we all couldn't wait for the warmer weather. Our conversation turned to memories of the beach and the shore. We are less than an hour away from the Atlantic Ocean. And most people that I've ever known in NJ had always taken great advantage of this. The coastline of NJ is quite stunning. Our state of NJ takes a lot of heat for some reason. Jokes, wisecracks, etc. Yet so many people want to move here and do. I know our license plates say

"The Garden State" but if those monikers were applied today? I doubt we would have earned that one, there's so much urban growth here. Then again we also have the beaches of New Jersey which all seem to be famous. Wildwood has a boardwalk and it's share of fans, Seaside Heights also has a boardwalk and was famous well before the show (Jersey Shore) started. Asbury Park has the Stone Pony where Bruce Springsteen treated people to impromptu appearances before and after he was famous. Jon Bon Jovi was yet another guest. And let's not forget Atlantic City. Also popular long before the show "Boardwalk Empire" and the casinos. Some people now call us the Soprano state.

I knew people from California who couldn't wait to visit NJ just so they could visit the Jersey shore! All the way from California. They have lovely oceans in California too, but the fun we always had at the Jersey shore? Nothing like it. I

then had my idea for the coasters. I always take my digital camera with me when we go to the beach. My brother has a boat that he keeps docked in Long Beach Island a beautiful stretch of Beach in NJ. Since he is there every weekend, (no matter what the weather is) we can go and visit him any time we would like. Naturally when I go I am forever snapping shots of all things ocean. I decoupage some pictures onto glass and frame them, so that during times like this, when our skies are grey and the temperatures are staying steady in the 20s and below? I can look at the pictures, pull up the warm memories and remind myself that scenes like this are only a couple of months away.

For this project I used some of my own digital images of Starfish, but you can certainly find pictures and make copies of these magical creatures anywhere! You can also use sea horses. Postcards can be copied to use for decoupage, there are no shortages of these.

You can also cheat on these a little bit. You can go to the craft store and buy real starfish. They are no longer living but they are quite lovely just the same. I see them in wreaths all the time. You can also buy sand, and you can go out into your yard or a nearby forest or park and take a few sprigs of live Blue spruce. The needles are feathery and long, and the blue green color reminds me of water. On a piece of waxed paper you can lay the sand down so you can't see the table beneath it. Arrange your starfish, with shells if you want and the branches of blue spruce, and snap away. You could also add pearls or gems or sea glass. If you know a little about photo shop you can do an artistic prompt on the pictures by using the watercolor image. Print them out on your copier, and take them to the photocopy store and make as many copies (and extras) as you need.

Here is the supply list for this project.

- Bowl of hot soapy water
- Lint free cloth
- Pictures of an ocean themed nature (make sure to make laser copies of them)
- Cork backing-you can also use sheets of adhesive backed felt available in the craft store.
- Long Flat artists paint brush (I would designate one brush for glue since it will get messy)
- High gloss varnish (I used Triple Thick by Deco art from the jar)
- If giving as a gift, sheer ribbon or raffia.
- E 6000 Glue
- Sand (available in craft store)
- Blue and or green very fine glitter
- 4 White Porcelain Tiles (4 x 4 inches) available in any Large Box Home Store
- Decoupage Glue
- Heavy grit nail file
- Shallow dish of water
- Hard brayer
- Zinsser™ Cover Stain- oil based (available at hardware stores)

Here are the instructions for making these coasters.

1. Wash the tiles in hot soapy water. This will remove any residue on them. Dry.

2. In a well-ventilated area, spray the tiles with Zinsser™ cover stain. Best to spray this outside, weather permitting. Let this dry for at least an hour. While this is drying, cut your square image out. If you can dry this in a closed off room with the heat on it will more quickly.

3. When the Zinsser™ is dry place decoupage glue over the whole front of your tile. Dip your image into the shallow dish of water, then dab it on your lint free cloth to remove excess water and place image face up on the tile, over the glue.

4. Fold the edges around the tile. (When this dries you will tear off the excess.)

5. If your image is crooked you can straighten it now. This is another good reason to dip the image in water before applying it to the tile. Now use your brayer to move all excess glue and any air bubbles out. Start in the center and roll the brayer out to the closest edge. Let this dry as you repeat these steps with your other tiles. Give each tile about a half an hour to dry depending on humidity level.

6. Now tear away any excess paper around the tile edges. Use your nail file to file away any paper that is still there.

7. Add 3 more coats of decoupage glue allowing tiles to dry between each coat.

8. Once you have finished applying the extra coats of decoupage glue, let the tiles dry in the driest room of your home.

9. Once they are dry, add the topcoat.

10. Dry according to instruction drying times

11. Place the dry tile on top of a sheet of cork (or adhesive backed felt) and make some marks with a pen along the outline so you'll know where to cut the cork or felt to fit the bottom of the tiles. Make sure none of the backing sticks out from under the tile.

12. Place E6000 glue all over the back of the tile. Press the cork directly over it making sure to turn the tile over and press it hard on the table. This way if there are any goops of glue, they will redistribute themselves around the base between the cork and tile. It will also secure the tile onto the cork. You can also use adhesive backed felt instead and just cut it and apply it.

13. Pour sand onto a piece of waxed paper. You can add blue and green glitter or yellow, gold or white into the sand if you would like. Put Glue E6000 all around the edges of the tile and place each side flatly in the sand/glitter. I have found this glue to hold permanently. So you don't find bits of sand on your furniture.

14. Once your glue is dry you can take ribbon or raffia and wrap around your stacked coasters. If you want, you can even add a tiny shell to the

center of the ribbon. You've now got either a lovely decorative and functional decoration for your room, or a thoughtful hostess gift to bring to your next party.

Bud Vase From Liquor Bottle

Have an interesting bottle around that you would like to reuse? But aren't sure quite how? Here's your chance to make it beautiful and functional. Why not use it as a mouthwash bottle? Or as I did here, a bud vase. You can find papers to match your bathroom décor and theme. I used some vintage wrapping paper over lavender Mulberry paper. And here's how I did it. This project is quite simple and if you would rather not use the polymer clay, you can still find a nice cork to fit and match the bottle. This was some type of hard liquor bottle that I found and liked the shape of, so I kept it.

Here's what I used on this project.

- Very Fine Glitter
- Lavender colored rice paper
- Pictures of Lilacs from wrapping paper (Wrapping paper will not run when it gets wet, so no need to make photo copies)
- Fine mister spray of water
- Hi gloss waterproof topcoat (I used Triple thick gel)
- Long flat artists brush (You can use brushes from a childs paint by number kit.)
- Shallow dish of water
- Lint free cloth
- Automotive sandpaper-this is very fine. Only to remove dust-not to actually sand.
- Decoupage scissors
- Decoupage glue
- Cork from wine bottle (If using for mouthwash bottle)

1. First, tear the Mulberry paper into sheets. There are fibers in this paper so allow it to tear where it will naturally. But make sure you take the hard edges off and place them to the side; we only want naturally uneven edges. Make sure you tear enough to cover the whole bottle.

2. The flat brush will make the mulberry paper adhere in a more uniform way. This paper is highly absorbent and is a great medium for use with decoupage. Cut out your images-whether they are floral, ocean, garden or aviary themed.

3. Apply decoupage glue to bottle where you will be laying the mulberry paper. Lay the mulberry paper over the area. Use your flat artists brush to apply more decoupage glue over top and to work out any air bubbles. This brush comes in particularly handy when you are working around curves and in the grooves of the neck of the bottle.

   Continue this process until you have covered the whole bottle. Leave this to dry for a half an hour.

4. Now we can begin to lay our images down where we would like. Always remember to do a dry run first. Which way will please you the most when you lay the images down on the bottle? When you are sure you have found the most appealing pattern, go ahead and decoupage them. Place decoupage glue on the bottle where you will be applying your image. Dip your image in the shallow dish of water and blot it on your lint free cloth. Lay it over the decoupage glue on the bottle. Use your fingers or a brayer to move the excess glue and air bubbles out from underneath the image.

   Continue to do this until you have finished decoupaging all of your images onto your bottle.

5. Let dry for a half an hour. Give it another coat of glue all over. Dry for 20 minutes and add one more coat of decoupage glue. (If you have a thicker image and you can still see a line where your images end, you will want to add enough additional coats of decoupage glue so that the images appear to be a part of the bottle and not something that was added on. You will want to sand very lightly, with automotive sandpaper after your final coat. This will remove any dust or hair particles that were airborne while you were drying-but have now attached themselves to your bottle.

   Give each coat of decoupage glue at least 20 minutes to dry between coats. Touch it to see if it's tacky. If it is, you will want to wait until the surface feels smooth to the touch.

6. Add your topcoat now and allow it to dry according to the directions of your topcoat. I have used the Triple Thick Gel instead of the spray because I didn't want to have to go outside to use the spray. (It's still very chilly here!)

7. Just after you apply the topcoat and while its still wet, very lightly take some fine glitter and add a very light dusting over the piece. You only want this glitter to add a tiny high light to the piece. Some objects you want covered in glitter, but not this one. We are only going for an accent here. Some bathrooms have track lighting. Track lighting and glitter is a match made in heaven.

8. If possible put this piece just above a heat vent-though not on the vent, or indoors in direct sun light. Leave it to dry over night.

9. Re-use a cork from a wine bottle if you would like to use this bottle for

mouthwash. I took a sheer organza ribbon, tied it around the neck and added water and flowers.

Geisha Girl Butter Dish

Do you want to use decoupage for the most practical purposes? I bought this butter dish at a discount store for less than 5 dollars! That's unheard of around here. It was just a sturdy clear glass butter dish, until I got through with it. I also like this idea for the holidays. You may have a butter dish that you use all year round. But if you would like to follow these instructions for a particular holiday, you will find the possibilities endless. It's also very nice to have your guests ask where you got that lovely butter dish!

I found some images of Geisha girls on a charming site called Blackberry Designs. You can find the loveliest images on this site. If you don't know what to make you can always look around the site since you are sure to walk away feeling inspired.

For this project we are going to use Mulberry paper as the base. We will match the color of our mulberry paper with the colors of our image.

Here's a list of what we'll need to complete this project.

- Decoupage scissors
- Decoupage glue
- Images to decoupage
- Lint free cloth
- Nail File

- Mulberry paper (This is available in all craft stores and several stationery stores)
- Toothbrush with flexible head- used just for crafting. (Dollar store purchase)
- Drop Cloth
- Sponge brushes
- Acrylic paint
- Water based topcoat (water based polyurethane varnish)

We are going to be working strictly on the outside of this butter dish so that no glues or topcoats will ever come in contact with the butter. This is an item that should never see the inside of a dishwasher. Nor should it ever be submerged in water.

1. First, let's tear all of Mulberry paper into different sized strips. I took a whole sheet and wrapped it around the butter dish to see how much I would need. I then began tearing. Put the sharp straight edges into a separate pile.

2. Cut out your images. I am going with an oriental theme on this dish so I will cut the geisha girls out. Place them aside.

3. Wash your glass butter dish with hot soapy water and rinse well. Dry.

4. Put decoupage glue onto one area of the butter dish. Don't cover the whole area, rather work in small area's first. Since you are working with Mulberry paper you don't have to make sure the paper is all going in the right direction. You should overlap pieces of it and lay it in any direction you want. Use both large and small pieces. The one caution I have is that you don't want to run your brush over the paper too often since it is delicate and it could roll up or tear. So place the paper, brush a layer of deco glue over it and move on. Repeat this until the whole outside of the butter dish top is covered. You will need to overlap the edges of your dish. That's ok, since we'll be filing that away when it dries.

5. The technique that you are doing on the bottom of the butter dish is actually referred to as Reverse Decoupage. Take your image, dip it in water and lay it face up *underneath* the butter dish. As you look down at the butter dish-the image will be facing up so you can see it clearly. You don't want to see the back of the image. You only need to wait for about 20 minutes for this process to dry. Then begin adding the

Mulberry paper over the back of the image on the bottom of the dish. We are trying to go for the effect of getting down to that last pat of butter, and seeing your image looking up at us. The mulberry paper will be behind your image.

6. Let it dry for at least a half an hour. The drying process always depends on humidity levels. During the cooler months these projects will dry faster when placed near a heat vent. Touch it to see if it's dry.

7. Once your piece has dried, you can now begin to decoupage the images onto your piece. As always you will want to do a dry run to make sure all the pieces look nice before you place them on permanently. Once you have a good idea of where you will place your images begin to decoupage.

8. Place some decoupage glue where you will be placing your image. Dip your image in water and dab it dry. Then lay it over the wet glue. Which is actually over the Mulberry paper.

    Continue this process around your butter dish until you are finished. When are done covering your dish you should leave it in a dry room to dry for several hours. Overnight would be best.

9. You will now get your paint, flexible toothbrush, and your drop cloth. Take the toothbrush and dip it in paint. Run your thumb along the edges of the toothbrush so that the paint splatters. You may want to practice this technique first on your drop cloth. You can also do it inside a box where it won't matter where the splatter goes. You just want to get a feel for working with the toothbrush. You can also make your paint more fluid by adding water to it. Or you can keep it the same thickness. It's all about personal preference. I tend to go with a darker color since it adds depth to the piece. Start with a light dap of paint on the brush and run your finger over it lightly to see how the splatters or dots come out. Let the piece dry. Preferably near a heater or sunny window.

10. Use a topcoat. The water based polyurethane varnish comes in a small can and can easily be applied using a sponge brush. Make sure it's a clean dry sponge brush with no lint or hair on it. This will water proof your piece keeping it fresh in the humid environment of your refrigerator. A clean damp cloth is all that is required to clean the outside, while a damp cloth with soap on it will be required to clean the base of the dish where the butter goes. And you're done!

Vintage Suitcase/Decoupage over Oil Paints

There is just something about an old suitcase. The keys, the lovely old fashioned inside complete with the little pockets. The energy this suitcase must carry. Has it been all around the world or just on a few vacations to the shore? We know that someone had it for a long time. That it was probably used for the happiest times, trips to destinations that help us learn about life and sometimes grow closer to our families. The Salvation Army is a good source for finding these unwanted pieces of luggage.

With all of this in mind I wanted to give this old hard plastic suitcase a new life. It's in great condition for its age. The keys are still with it and there are no tears or stains on the inside lining.

Since the plastic is pitted like an orange the best way to paint this will be to stipple it, with stipple brushes. The oil paints that you normally use for stencils will be perfect for this project. As I tried to shop for these oil paints, I noticed that one of the larger craft stores was no longer carrying them-while one of the other large craft stores had them in abundance. I am using the stencil paints for this project. So here is what you will need.

I also need to mention that since we are working with oil paints this project will take a longer time to dry. This is not a project you can do in an afternoon. Rather you will need to do it in steps.

These suitcases are lovely pieces to keep your blankets in; jewelry, off-season clothes or you can simply display them in an empty corner or entranceway. There are some inventive types who sell them as pet beds too!

The following items will be needed for this project.

- Zinsser™ oil based cover stain
- Low tack blue painters tape
- Hard stipple brushes 1 for each color (do not buy the cheap kids set)
- Pots of stencil paints
- Gesso (white)
- Brush cleaner
- Decoupage scissors
- Decoupage glue
- Sponge brushes
- Images of your choice
- Water based top coat
- Hard plastic Suitcase-the size is up to you and it does not have to be vintage. I have seen people use the hard make up cases to create some beautiful decoupaged projects.

Before you begin I would like to suggest that you take your images to the store with you if you are going to buy these oil paints. You will want to see that the colors of the paints match or compliment the colors in your images. Sometimes what looks like peach at home will actually look a little pinker in the daylight.

1. Use your low tack blue painters tape on all of the hardware. You don't have to be too fussy with this because the paint won't stay on the hardware for long even if it does manage to come in contact with it.

Because you aren't base coating the metal properly you can just scratch off any residual paint that may come in contact with the hardware. The tape tears very easily.

2. We are now going to spray the Zinsser™ all around the outside of the suitcase. This has to be done outside so that you'll have proper ventilation. I keep a large box and a flat piece of drop cloth handy so that I don't get any paint on the driveway. The Zinsser™ dries quickly and while it is drying you will want to cut out your images.

3. Cut out your images. Even though I have been doing decoupage for years, I only recently learned a nifty trick. Since this project is larger I am going to require more images, so I took 3 copies with the images on them and lined them up perfectly. (4 were too many.) Once I had them in perfect alignment I put pieces of tape at the top, and on the side folding the tape over the edges. This kept the papers all aligned as I cut 3 images at a time. I was so excited! I am sure that some clever decoupour has done this in the past. But I was not aware of it so I was quite proud of myself. Sharp decoupage scissors are crucial though.

4. Paint your suitcase with the oil paints. Before you begin to pounce the stencil paint on the suitcase, you are going to want to do a dry run and place your images on the suitcase in a way that pleases you. It's so important to do this first. This way you can see how your final project will look before you commit the images to the piece with the decoupage glue. To use the stipple brush, simply dab it into the little plastic well of stencil paint and begin to pounce it onto the surface of the suitcase. This is going to take some time. So be prepared to sit in the same place for a while. You will need to be comfortable in your seat. You will want to blend the colors along the edges. I am starting with the white (or the lightest color first) because I am going to blend the other colors over top of it. I am going for a springtime look and the white will help the other colors blend together for a pastel effect. I am going to be using a very dark purple, a vivid pink and a dark cherry. I rubbed my brush into the paint to make sure it was all covered and the paint had gotten up into the bristles, then I began to pounce. All you do with pouncing is just bounce the brush down onto the surface again and again. Since I am using a white on white, (the white stencil paint over the white Zinsser) I can't really see where I am painting unless I hold the suitcase in very bright light. But even if I miss a spot here and there, it will be fine. We'll be adding so much paint that the whole surface will be covered. Since this is a repetitive movement on your

arm you can become ambidextrous just for today. Use your other arm for a while to give your muscles a rest. This is not an exact type of painting so your other arm will work just fine. Work on one side of your project at a time. You will probably not finish painting in one sitting so make sure you keep all of your colors together so you don't go back to your project in a few days scratching your head wondering which colors you used.

5. Once you have the whole surface covered in the white or light paint, you can now begin to add some colors. This is fun! You need to pick up a smaller stipple brush, and dip it into one of the other colors. I started with purple. The dark purple over the white is allowing me to make my shade go anywhere from lavender to a dark purple. I don't want it that dark but it's nice that I can add so much depth by keeping some areas light and some darker. That's the best thing about oil paints, I think. That they don't dry quickly. Perfect for this project. It's also ok to add pink into the purple, but do not blend more than 3 colors. This could start to muddy your project. I'm not an oil painter, so some of you out there know a lot more than I do, and know what you can and can't do, I am just suggesting that it's best to stick to 3 colors for this project. I made the area heavy in lavender on one end, heavy in pink on the other and a combination of the two in between. Once in a while I would again add the white oil paint to lighten up a spot that had gotten too dark. Even though I am using one brush per color, the other colors will get onto your brushes. That's ok. It all works.

6. When you are all done with this side of your project, you will want to place the suitcase in a very warm dry room. I put mine in our guest bathroom right next to the heat vent. I shut the doors so that the environment was very dry. This part may be hard to believe but the suitcase needs to dry (cure) for at least two weeks before you begin the decoupaging. The humidity levels will dictate the actual amount of time. If it's drying in any conditions other than arid, you will need yet another week to dry it. Unless you can keep it in sealed room with your clothes dryer-you will need to let it cure for at least 2 weeks.

7. Now it's time to decoupage. I have my images all cut out and in front of me. Place decoupage glue down only on the area where you will be putting your first image. Dip your image in water; lay it briefly over your lint free cloth so it absorbs the excess water. Place your image down over the glue. Repeat these steps all over your suitcase. Always place your image in water before laying it over the decoupage glue on your

surface. The weight from the water will help images sink into the "pits" or any scratches on the suitcase. Once you place your wet image over the area where you have placed the decoupage glue you will want to use your sponge brush in very small gentle strokes, from the center of your image out.   Instead of laying the image down and using the sponge brush like a paintbrush, making a wide sweeping stroke over the whole image you will work in one little section of the image at a time, from the center of the image out. Once you are done with decoupaging one side of your suitcase, apply a fresh layer of decoupage glue over the whole surface. Let that dry as you work on the other side following all the steps mentioned after the number 6 above.

8. When your project is complete you will want to add 4 to 10 more coats of decoupage glue to whole surface of your piece. I know there are some instructors that would tell you and exact amount of layers of decoupage glue, but I have found that it depends on the thickness of the paper you are working with. The idea is to make it look like the images are painted onto the suitcase. If you're using images from a napkin, that look will be achieved much faster than if you were using card stock.

9. After two days of drying time you can now top coat the piece. Using your sponge brush you can apply the topcoat just like you would any paint. Cover your whole surface. You may want to apply 2 coats but you will not need more than that.

Faux Stained Glass Votive

Think of any piece of glass that you have. An old window. A lovely jar or bottle that you just didn't want to throw away. Even a drinking glass. This project can be done on any glass surface. It will make it much easier to do if you're working on a flat surface though. You may even want to go to your local hardware store and start out with a clear pane of glass for practice. Or have glass cut to fit inside one of your favorite frames. Do you have any old frames around with glass in them? You can decoupage directly onto the glass then place your artwork right back in the frame! The faux lead product will more than likely be the most difficult challenge of this piece. But then again, it only requires practice like anything of beauty.

The piece I am working on measures 6 inches around the bottom and 4 inches around the top. It's 6 inches tall. I'm not sure where I got this piece of glass but I can surely put a candle in it when we are done to softly light our patio table at night.

Here is what we are going to need:

- Decoupage glue Decoupage scissors
- Assorted colors of tissue and mulberry paper (Mulberry paper is available in craft and art stores as well as some stationery stores.
- A couple of reseal able plastic sandwich bags
- A simple stained glass pattern (available from books in your library or on line)
- 2 copies of the stained glass pattern (Most libraries have copy machines in them if you don't want to take the book out.)
- Simulated liquid leading by Plaid™ (available in craft store and on line)
- Triple Thick™ top coat (the one in the jar) available at the craft store
- A dull lead pencil
- A dry erase marker
- Small artists paint brush (the kind from the paint by number kits.)

1. First we are going to decide which colors look best for each piece. For example, I am working with a swan pattern. I'll want blue and green for the background since these are the shades of water. I'll use white and off white for the swan. A rust color for one part of the beak and orange for another section of the beak. An olive color for the eye.

   We are going to have to stay somewhat organized for this project. Organization is not my forte. So please bear with me as I try to keep things in order. This is where the zip lock bags will come in handy. We will keep the separate pieces of papers that we need in separate bags. This will save you a lot of time.

2. Trace out the colors that you will want for your pieces. For instance, for the beak I will take the orange mulberry paper and I will place it _over_ the copy of the stained glass pattern. With your dull lead pencil trace the line over the mulberry paper. The paper is sheer so make sure your pencil is dull.

3. When you are done tracing the shape, cut it out and place it into a zip lock bag. You do not need to make these cut outs the exact size. As a matter of fact you will want to keep in mind that you will be adding the

faux solder over all of the lines in your pattern.

4. You will repeat this same process for all of the pieces of your pattern, depending on what colors you want to use with what section of your pattern. My way of staying organized is to put the colors or cut outs meant for the swan's body in one zip lock, the cut out's for the water in another and the smaller facial items in yet another. This also prevents them from blowing away.

5. Now, tape the pattern to the inside of the glass or behind it if you're working on a pane or plate.

6. Decoupage your cut pieces over top of it. The process is simple. You will apply decoupage glue to the outside of your glass using a thin coat. Then apply the proper piece of tissue paper that you have cut out to fit over the pattern. Apply the papers as if you were working on a puzzle. Each piece has it's own designated place. Do *not* run your brush over what you have just placed down. This will bring the flimsy paper right back up to your brush. But you can use our brush to secure the paper onto the glass. Use light dabs of the brush over the paper. Let it settle and dry where it is.

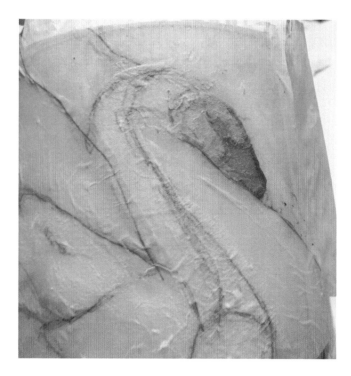

As you can see this doesn't look that attractive yet. If you're looking at your own piece and thinking it's a mess, no worries. It will look lovely when you're done.

Once you are finished with the first layer of your papers, you may find that some areas look too sheer. Or the color isn't as intense as you would like. Just add more of the same color paper over those areas. Although you also want to keep in mind that you may want to keep it sheer so that a soft candle glow can shine through. It's fine if it looks lumpy.

7. If you are working on a 3 dimensional piece like the one I am showing, you can repeat your pattern on the back part of the piece or extend the larger images around the back as I did. Instead of repeating the swan pattern onto the back of this project, I simply carried the water theme around the back.

8. It is crucial to dry this project thoroughly. I gave my piece a whole day to dry. Once the piece is dry we can begin to apply the faux lead. This product doesn't contain any lead by the way. I used to take classes and work on authentic stained glass projects so I have some experience working with actual soldering techniques. Faux soldering is a lot easier and there's no burning! That said you might want to practice on a piece of waxed paper. You can put waxed paper over a piece of newspaper, a comic or an ad, and attempt to outline it so you can see how the faux

solder comes out. If you are good at putting piping on a cake then you are probably going to do very well with this technique.

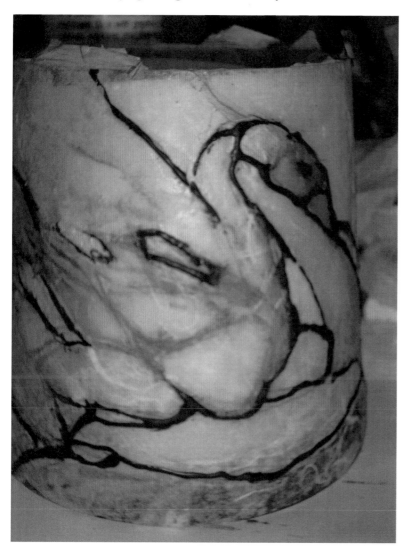

When you feel secure with your (Faux) soldering abilities go ahead and apply the solder over all of the lines on your pattern like you see in the preceding picture. The faux solder will dry faster than you would think but follow the instructions on the label as humidity levels will always affect dry time.

9. Once it's dry you can apply your topcoat. The reason I am using the product called Triple Thick (in the jar) is because as you will see when you open the jar, it is quite thick and it dries to the highest gloss possible. The only times I've seen a higher gloss on a project is after I've use a two-part epoxy topcoat. If you are working on a flat surface you can take a sponge brush and begin to paint the Triple Thick over your surface. Do not go over a spot again and again. This product can become lumpy if you over do it. So put enough of it on your brush to begin with and work

in a small area. If you are working on a 3 dimensional surface you will want to lay it flat. It's best to work on only one side at a time. And you don't want the product to drip down. What I did was placed my votive on its side over a piece of waxed paper. I then placed two old books along side of it. The books had to be books I wasn't worried about ruining. A lot of us crafters have plenty of those around. I did this so the votive wouldn't roll one way or another. I then applied the Triple Thick™ over the one side. Allowed it to dry. Then applied it to the other side. Don't worry about flattening out the faux solder. As long as your Triple Thick has dried you will be protected.

Here's the completed project in the dark.

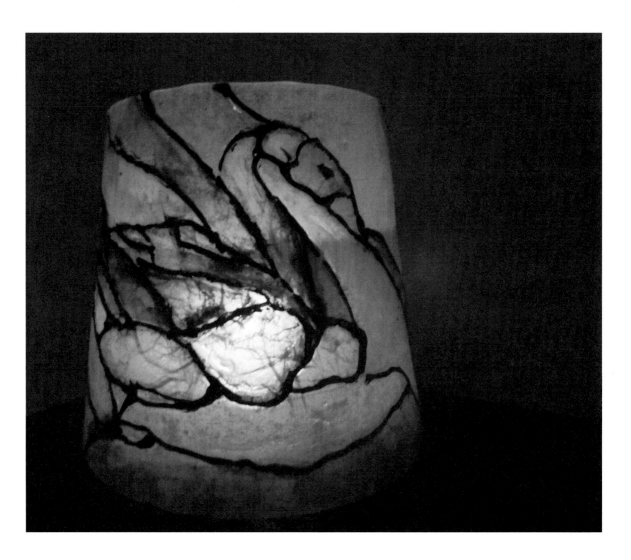

Upcycled Wicker Basket

Probably my favorite aspect of doing decoupage is turning something old into something new. Or at least making something look new. I had this old pink wicker basket sitting around. The color pink on it was out of date and faded to boot. The basket even had some imperfections but I knew how to take care of that! I'll show you how to fix that too.

Here is a list of what we'll need to get this project done and looking new and pretty in a short amount of time. This basket will probably be around for years once you finish it. So find some decorative napkins that you really like. There are some very pretty paper napkins available today.

Sometimes you will find them in grocery stores, but you can also find them in home goods stores, stationery stores and of course on line. I am using two napkins that are similar in color. One has lovely handwritten script on it, and the other has butterflies that I know will compliment the script napkins. It's all right if you would prefer to use just one very pretty napkin. I've used napkins that are one big bold hydrangea print all over some of my baskets. They turn out quite unique. Another added bonus is that you can select colors to match the room you are decorating.

Here is our supply list.

- Cream colored spray paint (Unless you're working with a new wicker basket)
- Fine Mister of water Wicker basket
- Decoupage glue
- Decorative napkins (if using a napkin with Script in the background it's best to use a second print of napkins with a solid feature like a flower or butterfly.
- Fine art paintbrush (not a sponge brush)
- Small container of water
- Flat head paint brush
- Topcoat (I used Triple Thick ™ in the jar)
- *Clear Wallpaper paste - you will need this if your basket has a pattern other than a simple weave.
- *Optional Brilliant glitter or Mica.

1. Spray paint your basket inside and out. Let Dry. Usually two coats works best.

2. If you are using napkins with a script pattern or any fine pattern that will be uses as your first (background) layer, you will want to apply those napkins first. Tear off the hard edges on the napkin. Apply decoupage glue to the section of the basket that you will be working on first. As much as you can, lay the napkin straight over the decoupage glue. Take your mister of water and spritz the napkin. This will cause it to sink into the crevices. Use the fine tipped paint brush to very gently push the napkin down into the crevices. Don't paint with the brush, just use it to push the paper down where needed. Sometimes the mist of water alone will cause the paper to sink into the crannies. (Don't you love that word?) Repeat this step all around your basket until you have covered the whole basket. It's ok to leave some napkin to over lap on the top or bottom. When it's dry you can easily tear that away.

3. When you are applying your second type of napkin image you will want to first tear it down the center in between the two-mirrored images. Use a wet paintbrush (one that does not have decoupage glue on it) to paint a thin line of water across the seam that separates the upside down image from the right side up one. This allows you to tear the napkin very easily. (Most napkins have 3 layers. Do not separate the napkins layers.)

4. Take your decoupage glue and apply it to the area of the basket where you will be placing your napkin only. With the fine tipped artists brush you will be able to get into the nooks more easily. Make sure you press deeply into these areas. You can cut the images out if you would like. But since we are using napkins and they are sheer, it's not necessary.

5. Gently place your half a napkin down where you just placed your decoupage glue. When you are happy with the placement take your mister of water and spray a light coat of water (do not saturate) over the napkin. Make sure the sprayer is set to the finest mist. You'll notice the napkin sinking into the crevices of the weave from the weight of the water. This is why we are not using a sponge brush; the small fine artists brush is better able to get the glue down into the crevices.

6. Repeat steps 2 through 4 covering the whole basket on the outside only. You may want to cover the bottom too. Simply wait until the top of your basket is dry and turn it upside down to repeat the above steps. Let Dry. Do not worry if there are some holes poking through your piece. Do not worry if the sides are not lined up, or if you accidentally did tear the napkins while decoupaging them onto your

basket. We can handle all of that in our next step.

7. Now that your piece is dry, let's have a look around the whole thing. Do you see any spots where you can see through the basket? Any holes? If so take your decoupage scissors and cut out a few images from your napkin. Since I first used a napkin that was all script, I will now cut out butterflies from my complimentary (second) set of napkins. These will work like band aids although they will be permanent. The reason I am using two different napkins is so that I can add some variety to my theme while covering up some of the inevitable bare or torn spots.

8. Take your decoupage glue and place it using the same artists brush over the areas you would like cover up. Place your image over it.

   Since you already have a base on the basket (the first layer of napkins) you won't need the mist of water. But very gently run your brush over the image to flatten it over the area. When decoupaging it's always important to make sure the ends are completely glued down.

9. Let Dry for at least an hour.

10. Once your piece is dry apply at least 5 new coats of decoupage glue all around your basket. Letting dry between each coat. It usually takes a half an hour for each coat to dry. If it's humid outside try putting your piece in a room where you can shut the door and keep the windows closed. Heat and Air conditioning are always a big help as is indoor sunlight.

    *One caveat about step number 11. If you have a solid weave on your wicker basket, meaning there are no decorative openings in the piece, you can skip this step.

11. Now that all layers have dried, you will want to reinforce the inside of your basket with the clear drying wallpaper paste. You can use the fine artists brush to apply this all around the inside. Let Dry. It's not necessary to apply more than one coat unless you use this basket for reasons other than small trash pieces.

    This will dry quite hard and prevent your work of art from tearing. Let this dry but let's let it dry over night.

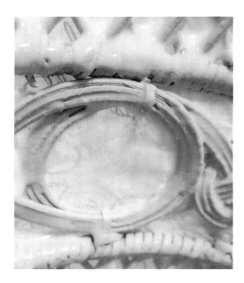

12. Now for our final step. I am going to use triple thick brush on topcoat. This is incredibly shiny and gives your piece a lot of depth. Since I love a little glitter under the glow of the track lighting in the bathroom, I am going to now sprinkle a smattering of mica all over the piece. I had to order Mica on line since I was having trouble finding it in craft stores. I love my glitter but there is something to be said for using Mica. The difference is negligible but you can see it. And now? You have an old wicker wastebasket that looks new again. Since I have always lined my wastebaskets, I have no worries about germs or bacteria on the old basket. And once you create something that you really like?
You may be hesitant to use it for trash! This is the before picture. Yuck, right?

Do you buy a new planner each year? Every other year? Or do you have one lying around that you would like to use but it just doesn't look the way you want it to? This project is just for you! Especially if you are an artist of any kind. Anyone with a creative aspect to their personality has to feel gypped by the limited styles of planners out there. They tend to look so business-like. Yet so many of us who are in creative occupations need a planner too! I especially like that this is a pleather (vinyl) planner that we will be upgrading! The instructions won't work for a leather planner so please don't use a leather planner for this particular project.

Did you know that you could paint vinyl? You need to use acrylic paint. I find that Gesso works very well too. I use the gesso as a base coat to cover the dark color of the planner but it also works to cover up any scratches that are on the surface. And helps the decoupage paper settle smoothly over the surface.

Here's what we will need to complete this project.

- At least 2 pieces of scrap book paper. I am working on a 5.5 by 8.5 size planner. If your planner is larger you may need two more pieces of scrapbook paper.
- Pleather planner
- Embellishments (found in the scrap book section of the craft store) I am using
- An adhesive flat-backed set of pearls.
- Scissors or paper cutter
- Shallow bowl of water
- Bowl of warm water
- Clean towel
- Clean rag
- Decoupage glue
- Sponge brushes (at least 2)
- White Gesso
- Brayer or Hard Squeegee
- 1/8th inch wide ribbon. (aprx a yard)
- Fabritaq ™ Fabric glue available in craft and fabric stores Ruler
- Images to compliment your scrap paper *(This is only if you want to decoupage further
- Decoupage scissors
- Acrylic paint to compliment your color theme or a paint marker Braided Ribbon
- Waxed Paper

I love my planner. I am a big note taker and I prefer a planner that I can hold in my hand, turn the pages and use my favorite pen in. Now? I like it even more since I can carry it into stores and have people ask me where I got it!

Here are the steps to completing your planner.

1. Paint the outside only of your planner using the gesso. You only need one

coat but do remember to wrap the paint around the inside of the planner. You can paint the fabric that's on the inside of your planner, the pieces that abut the zipper. You don't need special fabric paint either. Once the gesso dries you can paint the color of acrylic paint that you would like here. The Gesso dries quickly, within 20 minutes usually. It's convenient to use paint markers here too.

2. While your planner is drying you can cut your scrapbook paper to fit over the outside surface and around the inside of your planner. Not the whole inside. Look at it the same way you would when wrapping a shirt box. You want enough paper to go around the side and corners with a little on the inside. It is better to cut your paper too large than too small. You will need one sheet for the front of the planner and one sheet for the back. As for the width, you will want to remember to cover the binding. So if your planner measures 5 inches wide, and the binder *the spine of your planner-is 2 inches wide, you'll cut your paper to make sure it's 7 inches wide.

3. Apply decoupage glue to the front of your planner making sure to get the decoupage glue on the binding. Also place a lot of decoupage glue on the inside of the planner where you will be folding your paper over. You do not want to get the glue in the zipper. But that's why you have your bowl of warm water and rag with you. If the front of your planner has a "lip or pocket" on it, you can go ahead and cover that up. Just lay your paper down as if you were working on a flat surface. We'll cover this with an embellishment later.

***If you get any glue on the zipper, just use the warm wet rag to thin it out. Wipe the zipper well. The first time I did this project, I got glue inside the zipper, and it took me hours of working with wet rags and a heat gun to get the zipper working again. If you don't have a zipper, you are one step ahead of the game! Dip your paper into the shallow dish of water making sure to wet the whole piece, and gently place it over the surface of your planner wrapping the side around the binder. You will want to bring the paper all the way to the back edge of the planner, right where it bends. In other words if you were to lay the planner flat down on it's front side looking directly at the back of the planner, you would not see the paper wrapping around the back. Use a brayer, a wallpaper spreader or even an old credit card and run it along the paper you just placed down.

You will remove air bubbles and extra glue that's just underneath the paper.

We don't want any wrinkles or air bubbles in this piece. Wrap the sides of the paper inside the planner on all sides. This gets messy, you will be using your fingers and you will want to make sure the papers sticks to the fabric piece just inside of the planner. Just like with wrapping gifts, you will want to cut little slits into the corners so the papers fold over smoothly. If your paper is too long just cut it before pressing it onto the fabric. Sometimes it takes a little extra work to keep that paper pressed down onto the fabric, but that's normal. Don't get discouraged.

4. Repeat this process on the back of your planner with one exception. Align the back piece of scrapbook paper with the edge of your front piece of paper that is covering the back binder. It doesn't have to be exact; you may want to overlap a little bit. You just don't want any spaces between the back piece and the front piece. No part of your planner should be visible.

5. Once you've completed covering the front and back of the planner, you'll want to let it dry. The best way to do this is to stand it up like a tent. Place it over the a strip of wax paper. That way it won't stick to the base it's sitting on.

6. Now that your planner is dry you have two options. You can continue to decoupage or simply add the topcoat and embellishments. If you do not wish to do any more decoupage on your piece, skip on to step 7. I chose to add a vintage women in the center. Then surrounded her with shabby roses. If you would like to do this step, here are the instructions. I went to Etsy and found the seller, "Glinda Collage Sheets" and purchased a few of them. This image came from the Vintage Ladies Collage sheet. I tore around the edges to make this into an oval shape. I knew I would be covering it with shabby roses I had cut out, so I wasn't that careful in making sure I cut oval perfectly. You may be using another image. In either case, put decoupage glue down over where you will be placing your image. Dip your image into the water, pat it dry on the lint free cloth and place it over the area on your planner where you just applied the glue. Use the same sponge brush that you used to apply the decoupage medium and go over the image making sure to get those edges flat down on the planner. Also make sure there are no air bubbles under your image. Follow these same instructions to add roses all around in an oval shape, overlapping the edge of the Vintage lady sheet. Once the flowers have been applied, make sure to add one more coat of decoupage medium to the whole surface of the planner. Front and back. Leaving it open like a tent to dry.

7. Apply a topcoat to the whole planner. I used a very high gloss coat called Triple thick on this. It's durable and the shine makes the images stand out that much more. Dry. A couple of hours near a heat vent or in a sunny window will do the trick.

8. Once this is all dry, we can now embellish! So you know I will only use Fabritaq™ on any materials. You may have your own favorite fabric glue but I've found this one to stick the fastest and hold the longest.

If you remember earlier in the directions I mentioned that my planner had a "lip" or pocket on the front of it. Here is where we will use the braided ribbon. You can also use a string of pearls if you're not going to be too rough on your planner. I am calling this braided ribbon but some people call it Gimp. I'm not sure which is correct so for the sake of keeping it simple, I'll say braided ribbon. I use a piece or the braided ribbon that is a quarter of an inch longer on each end, than my planner. *Before I cut it....* I added a large dollop of Fabritaq™ at the ends where I will be cutting it. I make sure to let it dry, which takes only about 15 to 20 minutes. I then cut it, place my fabric glue all along the back of the ribbon and place it down over my planner, vertically, covering that lip or pocket. On my planner this is a curved pocket so I gently placed the ribbon in the same curve. I made sure to add extra glue to the ends where I folded the ribbon over the inside of the planner and pressed the ends in firmly. Obviously you do not want the ribbon to interfere with the zipper, so you may need to cut it some more. Just make sure to use the Fabritaq™ to keep the ribbon from coming unbraided.

Before you forget you should also add the Fabritq™ to your left over ribbon ends to keep it from becoming unbraided

9. Finally, you will want to add the final touches. I found these pearl embellishments in the scrapbook section of the craft store. They come with adhesive already on them. They come in different shapes and colors. You simply peel them away from the clear plastic sheet they are on and adhere. I have another planner that is two years old that I used following all of the above steps and I'm happy to say, it's held up perfectly. I would add that with a planner as pretty as the one you are going to make, you will surely want to go out and buy yourself a special pen! Naturally you can make one with some polymer clay and glitter! But there are some lovely pens available for purchase in stationery stores, craft stores, clothing stores and on line.

Afterword

Patti's work can also be found in her Etsy store called Hydrangeapath.

For more information on her book, you can find her on the Facebook page, "Upcycle With Decoupage".

She also continues to add more instructional videos to her YouTube page, **patioelf**.

CPSIA information can be obtained
at www.ICGtesting.com
Printed in the USA
LVXC01n1129041113
359920LV00006B/14